# Poets of Munster

# Poets of Munster

*An Anthology*
*edited by Seán Dunne*

Anvil Press Poetry
BRANDON

Published in 1985
by Anvil Press Poetry Ltd
69 King George Street London SE10 8PX
and Brandon Book Publishers Ltd
Dingle Co. Kerry Ireland

Anvil Press Poetry acknowledges the financial
assistance of The Arts Council of Great Britain
in the publication of this book.
Brandon Book Publishers have been assisted by
both a publication grant and a contribution from
the Authors' Royalty Scheme of the Arts Council/
An Chomhairle Ealaíon, Dublin.

Set in Ehrhardt
by Fakenham Photosetting Ltd
Printed and bound in England
by The Camelot Press Ltd, Southampton

**British Library Cataloguing in Publication Data**

Poets of Munster: an anthology.
   1. English poetry—Irish authors  2. English
  poetry—20th century  3. English poetry—
  Ireland—Munster
  I. Dunne, Seán
  821'.912'0809419      PR8858

  ISBN 0–85646–121–0 Anvil
  ISBN 0–85646–122–9 Anvil pbk
  ISBN 0–86322–054–1 Brandon
  ISBN 0–86322–060–6 Brandon pbk

# Contents

## 6 CONTENTS

# CEOL CEANTAIR

Chuala sé an ceol i gcainteanna Dhún Chaoin,
Ni hiad na focail ach an fonn
A ghabhann trí bhlas is fuaimeanna na Mumhan,
An ceol a chloiseann an strainséir;
Ceol ceantair
Ná cloiseann lucht a labhartha,
Ceol nár chualasa riamh,
Toisc a ghiorracht dom is bhí,
Is mé bheith ar adhastar ag an mbrí.

Ceol a cloistear fós sa Mhumhain,
Fiú in áiteanna 'nar tréigeadh an chanúint.

SEÁN Ó RÍORDÁIN

*Music of a Place*

He heard the music in the speech of Dún Chaoin, not the words but the melody that goes through the accents and sounds of Munster, music the stranger hears; music of a place unheard by those who speak it, music I never heard because it was so close to me, its meaning holding me in its grip.

A music still heard in Munster, even in places where the dialect was abandoned.

# Introduction

HENRY PULLING, THE HERO of Graham Greene's *Travels With My Aunt*, says if he could have been a poet he would be content in a quite humble station, "to be recognised, if at all, as an English Mahony and to have celebrated Southwood as he celebrated Shandon." Mahony's 'The Bells of Shandon' is one of Pulling's favourite poems in Palgrave:

> There's a bell in Moscow
> While on tower and kiosk O
> In Santa Sophia
>    The Turkman gets:
> And loud in air
> Calls men to prayer
> From the tapering summits
>    Of tall minarets.
>
> Such empty phantom
> I freely grant them:
> But there is an anthem
>    More dear to me.
> 'Tis the bells of Shandon
> That sound so grand on
> The pleasant waters
>    Of the River Lee.

A. Norman Jeffares says 'The Bells of Shandon' should be sung "late at night in a Cork accent at a party" and, no doubt, many a party has been enlivened—or ruined, as the case may be—by the singing of that air. Its author, Francis Sylvester Mahony, was a native of Cork in the province of Munster. He wrote under the name of Father Prout, and his achievements, besides the *Reliques of Father Prout* for which he is best known, included translating

Moore's genteel melodies into Latin and Greek and publishing the result as *Moore's Plagiarisms.*

But it is as a native of Munster, the southernmost province of Ireland, that he is of interest here, and I mention him because 'The Bells of Shandon' is probably, for better or worse, the best-known poem by a Munster poet of the nineteenth century. Like much of the poetry produced in Ireland at that time, it touches only the most superficial pulse. Gaiety relieves it from the almost morbid heaviness which characterised so many of the poems written by Mahony's contemporaries.

Foremost among these was Jeremiah Joseph Callanan (1795–1829) whose translations from the Irish, unreliable as they are, gained him a considerable reputation. His versions are dated now and seem weighed down by the tone of the times:

> 'Tis down by the lake where the wild tree fringes its sides,
> The maid of my heart, the fair one of Heaven resides—
> I think as at eve she wanders its mazes along
> The birds go to sleep by the sweet wild twist of her song.

Callanan was one of those writers who spend their lives showing great promise. His career is a picture of unrealised potential, gripped as he was by a lethargy from which he could not escape and a sense of failure which dogged him to the end. He was unable to draw his talents together to produce a body of significant work, and it is as a provincial poet that he is best remembered. He died in Lisbon, an exile hoping to return to his native Cork.

Another Munster poet of that time was Thomas Davis (1814–1845) in whose company, together with Mangan and Ferguson, Yeats would later wish to be included. Editor of *The Nation*, Ireland's first truly national newspaper, and the author of many patriotic ballads, Davis expressed and inspired the popular mind of his time. His *Poems and Literary Essays* were published in 1846, two years before the botched rebellion led by the Young Irelanders whose organisation he had helped to found. His patriotic poem, 'Lament for the Death of Eoghan Ruadh O'Neill', was recited with marvellous venom by generations of Irish schoolchildren:

"Did they dare—did they dare, to slay Owen Roe O'Neill?"
"Yes, they slew with poison him they feared to meet with steel."
May God wither up their hearts! May their blood cease to flow!
May they walk in living death who poisoned Owen Roe!

Callanan, Davis, Mahony and the other minor Munster poets
never came near the standards reached by the best English poets
of the day. Callanan and Davis were both alive when Keats
composed his odes and Byron wrote *Don Juan*.

Yet this bleak view of Munster poetry in the last century needs
qualification. For in 1849 there appeared a remarkable book,
John O'Daly's *The Poets and Poetry of Munster*, subtitled 'A
Selection of Irish Songs by the Poets of the Eighteenth Century,
with Poetical Translations by James Clarence Mangan'. Man-
gan, the first Irish poet to strike a chord that sounds true to the
modern ear, was an avid translator from many languages with
most of which he had little or no acquaintance. His *Anthologia
Germanica* had appeared in 1845. Like a number of other modern
poets, Mangan wrote under different guises or masks, assuming
other voices to articulate his own or even, as some critics have
suggested, to avoid the fact that he had little original voice of his
own in the first place. Besides his own poems, a number of which
are very fine indeed, it is for his translations from the Irish that
he is best remembered.

*The Poets and Poetry of Munster* contains the work of twenty-five
poets and also includes a number of anonymous songs. The
poets include Aogáin Ó Rathaille (Egan O'Rahilly) from whose
work Yeats would later filch and who was called, with more
enthusiasm than objectivity, 'the Dante of Munster' by Daniel
Corkery. Ó Rathaille was the most important poet writing in
Irish in the eighteenth century, and his work was the last great
crack of the old Gaelic whip. Many later writers have translated
his poems and two of these translations, by Frank O'Connor, are
included in the present volume.

Other poets in Mangan's book included Seán Ó Tuama and
Aindrias MacCraith. Collectively known as *Filí na Máighe* (Poets
of the Mague), Ó Tuama and MacCraith are good examples of
what Mangan calls (in a phrase that could apply with equal
exactitude to himself) "the union of lofty genius with grovelling

propensities." Natives of County Limerick, these poets wrote at a time when poetry in Irish, and indeed the Irish language itself, was struggling for survival (a situation similar to that which exists in the last few Irish-speaking pockets of Munster today). A modern Limerick poet, Michael Hartnett, has written of such poets in 'A Visit to Croome 1745':

> I had walked a long time
> in the mud to hear
> an avalanche of turf fall down,
> fourteen miles in straw-roped overcoat
> passing for Irish all along the road
> now to hear a Gaelic court
> talk broken English of an English king.
> It was a long way
> to come for nothing.

For the poets translated by Mangan and included in John O'Daly's book, a shared community of listeners was no longer guaranteed. Like the language in which they wrote, the world as they knew it was usurped. The tone is often one of lament, as in 'An Abhainn Laoi' (The River Lee) by Eoghain Mac-Carthy, where mention is made of Donnchadh Mac-Carthaigh who "lost an estate of £60,000 per annum by his attachment to the unfortunate King James II and who died at Altona in 1734". MacCarthy's poem is tinged with sadness, far from "the pleasant waters of the river Lee" that run through Mahony's poem:

> And yet, though the Nobles and Priests
>   And Gaels of both high and low ranks
> Tell tales, and indulge in high feats
>   On its dark-green and flowery banks,
> I mourn for the great who are gone—
>   And who met by the Lee long ago—
> But most for the Church's true son
>   Who now in Altona lies low.
>         [*Mangan's translation*]

Mangan died in the year of the book's publication. Like Thomas Moore he was born over a grocer's shop, but there the similarity ends: his funeral, it is said, was attended by only three people.

*The Poets and Poetry of Munster* was a landmark on the road to the great revival of interest in Gaelic literature which began in the 1850s. Compared to the work of the Munster poets writing in English at the time of its appearance, it contains a depth of sincerity, an authenticity, which leaves them far behind. Aogán Ó Rathaille and his fellow poets may have been sad romantics lamenting the loss of an old order, but their work has a bitter, truthful force which is its best quality:

> Now I shall cease weeping these useless tears;
>   By Laune and Laine and Lee, diminished of their pride,
> I shall go after the heroes, ay, into the clay—
>   My fathers followed theirs before Christ was crucified.
>                              [*O'Connor's translation*]

O'Daly's book ensured that these poets would not be easily forgotten. When the fourth edition was published in 1925, J. P. Dalton wrote in his introduction: "The Munster Bards are happily in no need, at the present day, of an individual introduction to the reading public. . . . The poems of several of the Bards who shine in the brilliant Munster constellations have already been published in splendid editions; and the indications of the moment point to the likelihood that a similar tribute of appreciation will be rendered ere long even to the Bards of minor lustre." And in that same year, Daniel Corkery's *The Hidden Ireland* had appeared, a seminal and passionate study of the Munster poets which has often been criticised by writers and scholars whose comments on Corkery's book have been forgotten in a way the book itself has not. *The Hidden Ireland* was to have a wide influence (Hugh MacDiarmid, for example, acknowledged its importance in the development of his own ideas) but, at the time of its writing, "the brilliant Munster constellations" had become a dim flicker.

No other anthology of Munster poetry has been made from Mangan's time to this. Representative selections have appeared, from *Gems of the Cork Poets* (1883), to *Poetry and Legendary Ballads of the South of Ireland by Various Authors* (1894), and *Five Irish Poets* (1971), but as a substantial body of poems was not being produced, no substantial anthology could be produced either.

It is my belief that this situation has now changed, and an

anthology featuring the modern poets of Munster can now be safely made. Not all of the poets included in this book were actually born in Munster: Paul Durcan was born in Mayo and John Ennis in Westmeath, but all have been, to twist a phrase of Conor Cruise O'Brien's, involved in the Munster situation: in other words, they live there. At the same time, not all of the well-known poets who live there are included. The most significant absence in this respect is John Montague who lives in Cork, but whose work is so closely connected with Ulster that it would be flippant to include him in a book like this.

It would be merely an academic exercise to try and discover what these poets have in common. It is better that they be heard as individual voices than that any spurious homogeneity be forced upon them. Many of them are familiar, to a greater or lesser degree, with the Gaelic tradition, but the use to which they put their knowledge varies in each case. For some, it is a seam of language unwinding from the past, and the prosody of Gaelic poetry, its particular metres and, above all, its rich deployment of sound, infiltrates their work. It can be found in the dense sound-structures of Michael Hartnett's lyrics or in Patrick Galvin's energetic abuse:

> A pox and blight on the common jobber
> who ruined the trade of decent poets.
> I'll write no more and return to nature
> commune with horses and lie down with sheep.

For others, the Gaelic tradition is not so central an issue. The kind of Ireland dealt with by poets like Paul Durcan does not easily accommodate a hankering after a lost order. The Gaelic heritage can also be a burden, a blinker shielding the eye from a clear view of the present. Over-emphasis on the Gaelic past, and an accumulation of archaeological and historical details which often serve to evoke nostalgia rather than to confront the world, are reactionary and irrelevant devices, as sterile in their application as the academic discussion which dissects them.

Many readers in England and elsewhere overseas will not be familiar with the poets in this book. There are many reasons for this, but foremost among them is the fact that poetry from the Irish Republic has been almost completely ignored by critics in England for some years. Many of these poets are published by

Irish publishers, and many of those publishers feel it a waste of time sending review copies to English publications: they are seldom reviewed unless, as sometimes happens, the books are the result of co-publication with an English publisher. Not one poet from the Irish Republic is included in *The Oxford Book of Contemporary Verse*, to cite just one example, and this is a situation which recurs so often that one can only conclude that the editors of such books have simply not bothered to seek out the work of poets whose names are not heard within the pale of conventional taste. There is no sense of Southern Ireland as a spawning-ground for poetry. A cultural myopia is at work, with the result that many of the poets included here are as far removed from the gaze of many prominent English critics as Hugh MacDiarmid and David Jones were in their time. In each case, the reason is the same: these poets fail to fit the canon of contemporary taste. They come, in fact, from the wrong side of the tracks, though perhaps it would be more precise to say they come from the wrong side of the border. *Aquarius* is the only London journal to give them adequate space.

There are a number of poems in this book which surpass in quality the work of writers who are currently fashionable more for their slick use of images than for anything more lasting or profound. There is nothing superficial or slick, for example, in the poems of Thomas MacGreevy. A native of Tarbert, Co. Kerry, he fought in the First World War and went to stay in Paris for most of the 1920s and 30s. His friends included Joyce, Beckett and Arp, and it is the developments made by Eliot and Pound rather than any native inheritance which most influenced his work. An accomplished and adventurous craftsman, his use of the poetic line makes him one of the most radical Irish poets of his time. Wallace Stevens called MacGreevy's poems "memorabilia of someone I might have known, and they create for me something of the world and himself." Although Samuel Beckett considered his *Poems* (1934) the most important contribution to post-war Irish poetry, MacGreevy has not received the recognition he deserves. He was Director of the National Gallery in Dublin for some years, and his work often springs from a visual sense that's rare enough in Irish literature. Colours abound:

> You were there,
> and, in the half-light,
> the dark-green, touched with gold,
> of leaves;
> the light green, touched with gold,
> of clusters of grapes;
> and, crouching at the foot of a renaissance wall,
> a little cupid, in whitening stone,
> weeping over a lost poetry.

Although best known as a writer of short stories, Frank O'Connor made many translations from the Irish. Opinions differ as to their worth—the *Penguin Book of Irish Verse* includes over twenty, the Faber equivalent only five—but as Mangan's translations served to introduce many readers to Gaelic poetry in the last century, O'Connor's have served a similar function in this. His view of the older Munster poetry, as expressed in the preface to *Kings, Lords and Commons*, is of interest here: "In Connaught . . . there was genuine folk poetry, but in Munster the old world died in its sleep. The poetry of Egan O'Rahilly, David O'Bruadair and a hundred other peasant poets is that of the sleep-walker; their thought is so much of the old dead world that it is as though a veil had fallen between them and reality. When they speak English they are slaves: whining, cadging, labouring men, but behind the barrier of their own language they move with their heads in clouds of Romanticism." O'Connor translated enough from these poets to lead one to believe that his own head fitted comfortably into those same clouds. His translations from the Irish have been immensely popular.

Seán Ó Ríordáin wrote only in Irish. His knowledge of traditional forms, and his love for the culture of which the Irish language is a part, are matched by a mind which is contemporary in its concerns. The question of freedom is central to his work, where terror and doubt are often his only companions in a solipsistic world. He was one of a number of writers whose attitudes and methods broke through the suffocating smugness and lack of liveliness which characterised the Irish language movement up to the 1940s and which can still retard that movement today. A victim of tuberculosis, of which he was to die in

1977, Ó Ríordáin knew what it was to be isolated. He is *l'homme seul*, a stance which gives his work an immediate appeal to modern readers. He is considered by many to be the most significant poet writing in Irish since Aogáin Ó Rathaille. His completely personal attitude to language, and his constant questioning of situations which most people take for granted, mark him out not merely as an important poet writing in Irish but as one of the best European poets of his generation. Seán Ó Tuama has pointed out that Ó Ríordáin and others of his age were the first generation of writers in Irish since the seventeenth century to absorb naturally the contemporary life of Europe. If they knew their Ó Rathaille they also knew their Brecht, Maritain and Sartre, and this intellectual cosmopolitanism frees Ó Ríordáin's work from the insularity and provincialism which dogged many other poets writing in Irish. The claustrophobia which his poems reflect is often balanced by a sense of humour that borders on the grotesque.

Unlike his eighteenth-century namesake, Seán Ó Tuama avoids the attraction of alliterative excess. A playwright and distinguished literary scholar, his poems vary from reflective elegy to precise observations of nature. Like other poets writing in Irish, he believes that the Irish language offers a unique experience. He has written of Irish: "Not alone does it open up for us a life-experience of some 2,000 years, in poetry, song and stories, but by doing so it sharpens, for a majority of us, our awareness of a whole range of our own inherited patterns of thought, feeling and behaviour."

Robert O'Donoghue's poetry is of a different kind. Drama is never far away and his experience as a playwright shows in his tendency to write soliloquies. He has written few enough poems, most of them being an assumption of voices rather than a direct articulation of O'Donoghue's own: a bereaved girl, a prisoner, people hurt into poetry.

Patrick Galvin is another playwright-poet. Like O'Donoghue, he is a native of Cork. He absorbs that city into his work as only prose-writers like Corkery, O'Connor and Seán Ó Faoláin have previously done. His plays echo with Cork accents. His poems ring with memories and manifestations of Cork characters. He is also an excellent ballad-writer and singer, an interest reflected in his poems which often have the poignancy and humour of folk-songs.

Seán Lucy is yet another Cork poet. He is Professor of English at University College, Cork, and while his work is sometimes affected by a rather academic acquiescence to modernism ("the inner doomwalk of my generation"), he is at his best when this breaks down and a more passionate, personal voice breaks through. Such is the case with *Unfinished Sequence for Seán Ó Riada*. The most important innovator in Irish traditional music in this century, an original composer of merit and a figure who for a time seemed to embody in himself the possibility of a modern, Gaelic Ireland, Seán Ó Riada was a close friend of Lucy's and his death released a poetry of deeply-felt grief.

Desmond O'Grady has absorbed the lessons of modernism more naturally. His early friendship and correspondence with Ezra Pound was, as for so many others, a liberating influence. He has said of Pound: "I never felt whole when not in his company and I never left his company without feeling a renewed charge of creative strength." His poems are log-books of many journeys, whether to his native Limerick or to a Greek Island, among peasants, revolutionaries, poets, friends. Like Pound, he has written many translations, from the old Irish to Cavafy, and his own poems contain these resonances.

Brendan Kennelly, like Thomas MacGreevy, is a native of County Kerry. Where MacGreevy is cosmopolitan and, at times, impersonal, Kennelly is essentially local and warm. A prolific poet with over twenty collections to his credit, Kennelly is essentially a poet of celebration. He celebrates love, craftsmen, sportsmen, everyday life. His massive work *Cromwell* is a fascinating achievement. Filled with a manic energy, it acts as a net for a wide range of reference and experience. It is not possible to include any of it here as it is best read in full, but the poems in this book should give a good indication of Kennelly's talent. There are times when he seems to write with a kind of swaggering ease, but his poems at their best are well-made and accessible.

Michael Coady is also a celebrant of the local. He has written a number of poems about his native Carrick-on-Suir in County Tipperary, and he has been praised as a poet of the small town.

In a small way, he has created an Irish 'Spoon River' anthology. His humour has been compared to Gavin Ewart's, though Ewart's massive output is bulkier by far than Coady's.

With Michael Hartnett (Micheál Ó hAirtnéide) we arrive at one of the most interesting careers in modern Irish poetry. As mentioned earlier, he has written of the eighteenth-century poets who lived in his native County Limerick. His writing of them is not merely an act of homage: it is also the expression of a temperamental affinity. Hartnett began as a poet writing in English and his work in that language is elegantly wrought. He has written a version of the *Tao Te Ching* and excellent translations of Lorca's *Gypsy Ballads*. John Montague has called him "the most dedicated English poet to come so far from Munster, where the tradition of Gaelic poetry was strongest", and he was certainly considered to be among the best poets of his generation. Yet in 1976 he announced that he would no longer write in English: Irish was to be his medium from now on. Writing that year in the *Irish Times* of Seán Ó Tuama and Aindrias Mac-Craith, he said: "That they suffered for poetry, which at the best of times brings little reward, and at all times contempt, should not be forgotten. To keep Gaelic alive would be our best tribute to them: and we shall do that." This passionate commitment to the Irish language and a concomitant dissatisfaction with English was not merely the rejection of one language for another: it was also the rejection of a way of life.

Eiléan Ní Chuilleanáin's work is less public that Hartnett's. Her handling of classical themes—as in 'Odysseus Meets the Ghosts of the Women'—brings a freshness to jaded tales, and her knowledge of the Classics never intrudes on the marvellous details which dot her poems. She sees things from a startling point of view, and sometimes this unique outlook can lead to a poetry too personal to be shared. In her best work, this trap is avoided. Her poems are studded with objects which take on a life of their own. People are shadows, intruders on a canvas depicting still life.

Augustus Young has a lighter touch, and his long poem 'Mr Thackeray On Cork' is pleasantly readable. He is a fine satirist and has translated from the Irish. He is also capable of being topical, an ability once common among Irish poets but now difficult enough to find.

Pádraig J. Daly has written many poems dealing with the area around his native Dungarvan in County Waterford. He has a sense of injustice which can be stirred by the tribal memory of famine or emigration, or even by the scenes caught in a modern city street. At his best, he evokes places and moods in a manner that remains his own.

John Ennis is a poet whose work has been compared with many others, from Patrick Kavanagh and Dennis Devlin to Hart Crane. While such comparison is useful to a point, it is misleading if stretched too far. Ennis is an original voice. His poems contain many unusual words and while sometimes this leads to a prolix, exaggerated style where the language is heavier than the meaning, when it works, it works well. While his pictures of rural life fit into a fairly standard mode, his work can depict a savagery which sets it apart—in Irish poetry, at least. His poems on country life are not nostalgic flashbacks but part of an attempt to understand some greater theme, be it his father's death or the passing of innocence. He is a poet of unnerving directness: 'Birth at Airmount' deals with a theme unfortunately avoided by Irish writers. Again, his poems on the death of his father are detailed pictures of the process. With John Ennis, such explicit depiction is never morbid. It is part of a poet's effort to comprehend the event.

Paul Durcan is one of the most distinctive voices in recent Irish poetry. A writer of great range, he has written poems on countless aspects of Irish life, from the Godfathers of the I.R.A. to bishops, from the subservient rôle of women in Irish society to the loneliness of broken marriages. He is not simply the sum of his satires, however; a love-poet and a compassionate defender of the defenceless, he avoids what Anthony Cronin calls 'Celtic crepuscularities', and the Ireland of which he writes is never glamorised or subsumed beneath a poverty of historical detail. He is a kind of public radar, fixing on contradictions as they come into view.

Liam Murphy is a poet of suburban Ireland. His *Occasion of Wordshed* (1972) was seen in some quarters at the time of its publication as striking a new and important note. When many looked to the Mersey Beat for an idea of poetry and when pop culture led to pop poems, Murphy's poems fitted a particular slot. His tendency to use gimmicks, whether typographical or verbal, often took the reader's attention away from what the poem was actually saying. He is one of the few Irish poets genuinely to experiment with form, and his work in recent years has moved away from the superficiality of pop poetry.

Michael Davitt is one of a number of young poets whose work first came to prominence in the magazine *Innti*. His work is contemporary and experimental in the best sense. While for others the Irish language has been a romantic link with the past, for Davitt it is an essential and practical means of dealing with the present. In an interview with the *Sunday Independent* in 1982, he said: "My early poems were poems of discovery and amazement at the existence of the language. There were things I could express in Irish that weren't possible in English. It was almost a spiritual experience for me."

Maurice Riordan is one of a number of poets—Thomas McCarthy, Gregory O'Donoghue and Seán Dunne are others—who were students at University College, Cork in the 1970s. Outside of that fact, they have little else in common and their styles range from O'Donoghue's tightly-made images to McCarthy's expansive meditations on De Valera's Ireland or his father's death.

Nuala Ní Dhomhnaill is the most interesting of the younger poets writing in Irish. She was born in England and reared in County Tipperary. Her parents came from the Kerry Gaeltacht. Educated at University College, Cork, she has also lived in Turkey. Her work is characterised by a sensuousness and energy which made her book *An Dealg Droighin* one of the most exciting events in recent Irish poetry. Her work is finely crafted, and lines that on first appearance seem slackly constructed become, when examined, intricate skeins of sound. Which is, of course, in the best tradition of Gaelic poetry.

Aidan Murphy's poems are often accounts of individuals who, for one reason or another, have been set apart or hurt. His love-poems are among his best work; 'Friendship', for example. Brendan Kennelly has praised Murphy's "genuine power of suggestion and implication".

Dennis O'Driscoll is a poet fond of metaphor and he displays considerable ingenuity in its use. His use of metaphor is not, however, merely cleverness. His precise and vivid descriptions, whether of places or parts of the body, combine with the seriousness of his themes to produce a poetry deeply concerned with mortality. At times, his poems are written with a starkness that one usually associates with poetry from Eastern Europe. This is completely to his credit, and it prevents his work from falling into the trap of an easy lyricism.

Taking all these poets together, it can be seen that the differences between them are greater than the similarities. They have only Munster and poetry in common. Their themes and styles are as varied as the province itself and that, in the end, is how they must be seen. They are not a school but a group of different voices whose words deserve to be heard.

SEÁN DUNNE
*Cork, December 1983*

# A NOTE ON THE POEMS IN IRISH

ANTHOLOGIES OF MODERN Irish poetry usually exclude Irish-language writers completely. Of the poets included in this book, only four have written solely in Irish while a fifth, Hartnett, has written in English as well. Many others could have been included; of the fifty-four poets in *Nuafhili 3* (New Poets 3) published in 1979, over twenty came from Munster alone. Yet to give equal space to poets from both languages would be to present an unreal picture of the overall situation and, more to the point, would mean the exclusion of many poets writing in English.

The selection of poems in Irish, therefore, is representative rather than comprehensive. Rather than ignore the Irish language completely, I chose to include some of those who are considered to be among its finest poets. Verse translations accompany the poems in Irish, except in the case of Seán Ó Ríordáin, where my literal prose versions accompany the originals. Seán Ó Ríordáin's publisher, Caoimhín Ó Marcaigh, has kindly consented to the inclusion of my versions, despite his reservations about translations of Ó Ríordáin's poetry in general, and the adequacy of such plain versions to reflect the spirit of the poems.

S.D.

# Thomas MacGreevy

1893–1967

## DE CIVITATE HOMINUM

*to A.S.F.R.*

The morning sky glitters
Winter blue.
The earth is snow-white,
With the gleam snow-white answers to sunlight,
Save where shell-holes are new,
Black spots in the whiteness—

A Matisse ensemble.

The shadows of whitened tree stumps
Are another white.

And there are white bones.

Zillebeke Lake and Hooge,
Ice gray, gleam differently,

Like the silver shoes of the model.

The model is our world,
Our bitch of a world.
Those who live between wars may not know
But we who die between peaces
Whether we die or not.

It is very cold
And, what with my sensations
And my spick and span subaltern's uniform,
I might be the famous brass monkey,
The *nature morte* accessory.

*Morte . . . !*
'Tis still life that lives,
Not quick life—

There are fleece-white flowers of death
That unfold themselves prettily
About an airman

Who, high over Gheluvelt,
Is taking a morning look round,
All silk and silver
Up in the blue.

I hear the drone of an engine
And soft pounding puffs in the air
As the fleece-white flowers unfold.

I cannot tell which flower he has accepted
But suddenly there is a tremor,
A zigzag of lines against the blue
And he streams down
Into the white,
A delicate flame,

A stroke of orange in the morning's dress.

My sergeant says, very low, "Holy God!
'Tis a fearful death."

Holy God makes no reply
Yet.

# HOMAGE TO HIERONYMUS BOSCH

A woman with no face walked into the light;
A boy, in a brown-tree norfolk suit,
Holding on
Without hands
To her seeming skirt.

She stopped,
And he stopped,
And I, in terror, stopped, staring.

Then I saw a group of shadowy figures behind her.

It was a wild wet morning
But the little world was spinning on.

Liplessly, somehow, she addressed it:
*The book must be opened*
*And the park too.*

I might have tittered
But my teeth chattered
And I saw that the words, as they fell,
Lay, wriggling, on the ground.

There was a stir of wet wind
And the shadowy figures began to stir
When one I had thought dead
Filmed slowly out of his great effigy on a tomb near by
And they all shuddered
He bent as if to speak to the woman
But the nursery governor flew up out of the well of Saint
    Patrick,
Confiscated by his mistress,
And, his head bent,
Staring out over his spectacles,
And scratching the gravel furiously,

Hissed—
    The words went *pingg!* like bullets,
    Upwards, past his spectacles—
*Say nothing, I say, say nothing, say nothing!*
And he who had seemed to be coming to life
Gasped,
Began hysterically, to laugh and cry,
And, with a gesture of impotent and half-petulant despair,
Filmed back into his effigy again.

High above the Bank of Ireland
Unearthly music sounded,
Passing westwards.

Then, from the drains,
Small sewage rats slid out.
They numbered hundreds of hundreds, tens, thousands.
Each bowed obsequiously to the shadowy figures
Then turned and joined in a stomach dance with his brothers
    and sisters.
Being a multitude, they danced irregularly.
There was rat laughter,
Deeper here and there,
And occasionally she-rats grew hysterical.
The shadowy figures looked on, agonized.
The woman with no face gave a cry and collapsed.
The rats danced on her
And on the wriggling words
Smirking.
The nursery governor flew back into the well
With the little figure without hands in the brown-tree clothes.

# AODH RUADH Ó DOMHNAILL

*to Stiefán MacEnna*

*Juan de Juni* the priest said,
Each J becoming H;

*Berruguete*, he said,
And the G was aspirate;

*Ximenez*, he said then
And aspirated first and last.

But he never said
And—it seemed odd—he
Never had heard
The aspirated name
Of the centuries-dead
Bright-haired young man
Whose grave I sought.

All day I passed
In greatly built gloom
From dusty gilt tomb
Marvellously wrought
To tomb
Rubbing
At mouldy inscriptions
With fingers wetted with spit
And asking
Where I might find it
And failing.

Yet when
Unhurried—
    Not as at home
    Where heroes, hanged, are buried
    With non-commissioned officers' bored maledictions
    Quickly in the gaol yard—

They brought
His blackening body
Here
To rest
Princes came
Walking
Behind it

And all Valladolid knew
And out to Simancas all knew
Where they buried Red Hugh.


## HOMAGE TO MARCEL PROUST

*to Jean Thomas*

The sea gleamed deep blue in the sunlight
Through the different greens of the trees.
And the talk was of singing.
My mother, dressed in black, recalled a bright image from
    a song,
*Those endearing young charms,*
Miss Holly, wearing heliotrope, had a sad line,
*The waves still are singing to the shore.*
Then, as we came out from the edge of the wood,
The island lay dreaming in the sun across the bridge,
Even the white coastguard station had gone quietly to sleep—
    it was Sunday,
A chain on a ship at the pier
Rattled to silence,
Cries of children, playing, sounded faintly
And, musically, somewhere,
A young sailor of the island—

    He was tall
    And slim
    And curled, to the moustaches,
    And he wore ear-rings
    But often he was too ill to be at sea—

Was singing,
*Maid of Athens, ere we part* ...

Looking suddenly like a goddess
Miss Holly said, half-smiling,
"Listen ..."
And we stopped
In the sunlight
Listening ...

The young sailor is dead now.
Miss Holly also is dead.
And Byron ...
Home they've gone and

And the waves still are singing.


RECESSIONAL

In the bright broad Swiss glare I stand listening
To the outrageous roars
Of the Engelbergeraa
As it swirls down the gorge
And I think I am thinking
Of Roderick Hudson.
But, as I stand,
Time closes over sight,
And sound
Is drowned
By a long silvery roar
From the far ends of memory
Of a world I have left
And I find I am thinking:
Supposing I drowned now,
This tired, tiresome body,
Before flesh creases further,
Might, recovered, go, fair,
To be laid in Saint Lachtin's,

Near where once,
In tender, less glaring, island days
And ways
I could hear—
Where listeners still hear—
That far-away, dear
Roar
The long, silvery roar
Of Mal Bay.


## NOCTURNE OF THE SELF-EVIDENT PRESENCE

Fortunate,
Being inarticulate,
The alps
Rise
In ice
To heights
Of large stars
And little;
To courts
Beneath other courts
With walls of white starlight.
They have stars for pavements,
The valley is an area,
And I a servant,
A servant of servants,
Of metaphysical bereavements,
Staring up
Out of the gloom.

I see no immaculate feet on those pavements,
No winged forms,
Foreshortened,
As by Rubens or Domenichino,

Plashing the silvery air,
Hear no cars,

Elijah's or Apollo's
Dashing about
Up there.
I see alps, ice, stars and white starlight
In a dry, high silence.

## GIOCONDA

to Jean Lurçat

The hillsides were of rushing, silvered water,
Down,
And around,
And all across,
And about the white, gleaming tree-trunks,
Far as sensitive eyesight could see,
On both sides of the valley,
And beyond,
Everywhere,
The silvered swirling water!

The clouds,
Blue-gray
Lined with pink
And edged with silver,
Meditated.

The sun did not rise or set
Not being interested in the activities of politicians.

White manes tossed like spray.
Bluish snakes slid
Into the dissolution of a smile.

## ON THE DEATH OF JOSEPH DJUGASHVLI *ALIAS* STALIN

Of the three who threw the bomb,
None, we may like to think
Would poison a well.
We may also choose to believe
That one of them knows now
Whether he be with Lazarus or with Dives,
That the choice remains unchanging
Between Peter who wept bitterly
And Lucifer who has no tears.

# Frank O'Connor

1903–1966

## A SLEEPLESS NIGHT

I have thought long this wild wet night that brought no rest
    Though I have no gold to watch, or horned kine, or sheep—
A storm that made the wave cry out has stirred my breast;
    Neither dogfish nor periwinkle was once my meat.

Ah, if the men who knew me were but here tonight
    With their proud company that held me up secure,
Captains of Munster before their great defeat,
    Not long would Corkaguiney see my children poor.

MacCarthy stern and fearless that most upright man,
    MacCarthy of the Lee whose hearth is dark and cold,
MacCarthy of Kanturk and all his kindred gone—
    The heart within me breaks to think their tale is told.

The heart within my breast tonight is wild with grief
    Because, of all the haughty men who ruled this place,
North Munster and South Munster to the wave beneath,
    None lives, and where they lived lives now an alien race.

Ah, famous wave you sang the livelong night below;
    Small wonder if the noise set my wits wandering—
I swear if help could ever come to Ireland now
    I'd strangle in your raucous throat that song you sing.

*from the Irish of Aogáin Ó Rathaille*

## LAST LINES

*Because, like himself, O'Rahilly seemed the last*
*voice of feudalism, Yeats used the final line of this poem*
*for one of his own.*

I shall not call for help until they coffin me—
    What good for me to call when hope of help is gone?
Princes of Munster who would have heard my cry
    Will not rise from the dead because I am alone.

Mind shudders like a wave in this tempestuous mood,
    My bowels and my heart are pierced and filled with pain
To see our lands, our hills, our gentle neighbourhood,
    A plot where any English upstart stakes his claim.

The Shannon and the Liffey and the tuneful Lee,
    The Boyne and the Blackwater a sad music sing,
The waters of the west run red into the sea—
    No matter what be trumps, their knave will beat our king.

And I can never cease weeping these useless tears;
    I am a man oppressed, afflicted and undone
Who where he wanders mourning no companion hears
    Only some waterfall that has no cause to mourn.

Now I shall cease, death comes, and I must not delay
    By Laune and Laine and Lee, diminished of their pride,
I shall go after the heroes, ay, into the clay—
    My fathers followed theirs before Christ was crucified.

*from the Irish of Aogáin Ó Rathaille*

## ON THE DEATH OF HIS WIFE

I parted from my life last night,
   A woman's body sunk in clay:
The tender bosom that I loved
   Wrapped in a sheet they took away.

The heavy blossom that had lit
   The ancient boughs is tossed and blown;
Hers was the burden of delight
   That long had weighed the old tree down.

And I am left alone tonight
   And desolate is the world I see
For lovely was that woman's weight
   That even last night had lain on me.

Weeping I look upon the place
   Where she used to rest her head—
For yesterday her body's length
   Reposed upon you too, my bed.

Yesterday that smiling face
   Upon one side of you was laid
That could match the hazel bloom
   In its dark delicate sweet shade.

Maelva of the shadowy brows
   Was the mead-cask at my side;
Fairest of all flowers that grow
   Was the beauty that has died.

My body's self deserts me now,
   The half of me that was her own,
Since all I knew of brightness died
   Half of me lingers, half is gone.

The face that was like hawthorn bloom
　　Was my right foot and my right side;
And my right hand and my right eye
　　Were no more mine than hers who died.

Poor is the share of me that's left
　　Since half of me died with my wife;
I shudder at the words I speak;
　　Dear God, that girl was half my life.

And our first look was her first love;
　　No man had fondled ere I came
The little breasts so small and firm
　　And the long body like a flame.

For twenty years we shared a home,
　　Our converse milder with each year;
Eleven children in its time
　　Did that tall stately body bear.

It was the King of hosts and roads
　　Who snatched her from me in her prime:
Little she wished to leave alone
　　The man she loved before her time.

Now King of churches and of bells,
　　Though never raised to pledge a lie
That woman's hand—can it be true?—
　　No more beneath my head will lie.

*from the Irish of Muiredach Ó Dálaigh*

# Seán Ó Ríordáin

1917–1977


## ADHLACADH MO MHÁTHAR

Grian an Mheithimh in úllghort,
   Is siosarnach i síoda an tráthnóna,
Beach mhallaithe ag portaireacht
   Mar screadstracadh ar an nóinbhrat.

Seanalitir shalaithe á léamh agam,
   Le gach focaldeoch dar ólas
Pian bhinibeach ag dealgadh mo chléibhse,
   Do bhrúigh amach gach focal díobh a dheoir féin.

Do chuimhníos ar an láimh a dhein an scríbhinn,
   Lámh a bhí inaitheanta mar aghaidh,
Lámh a thál riamh cneastacht seana-Bhíobla,
   Lámh a bhí mar bhalsam is tú tinn.

Agus thit an Meitheamh siar isteach sa Gheimhreadh,
   Den úllghort deineadh reilig bhán cois abhann,
Is i lár na balbh-bháine i mo thimpeall
   Do liúigh os ard sa tsneachta an dúpholl,

*My Mother's Burial*

June sun in an orchard, a rustle in the silk of evening, an ill-tempered bee droning like a scream renting the evening-cloth.

Reading an old soiled letter, and with every word-drink I sip, a sharp pain pierces my side, each word pressing out its own tear.

I remembered the hand that made the writing, a hand distinguishable as a face, a hand which bestowed old Bible kindness, a hand that was balsam when you were ill.

And June fell back into winter, the orchard became a white cemetery by a river and in the middle of the dumb whiteness around me the black hole shouted out loud in the snow.

Gile gearrachaile lá a céad chomaoine,
  Gile abhlainne Dé Domhnaigh ar altóir,
Gile bainne ag sreangtheitheadh as na cíochaibh,
  Nuair a chuireadar mo mháthair, gile an fhóid.

Bhí m'aigne á sciúirseadh féin ag iarraidh
  An t-adhlacadh a bhlaiseadh go hiomlán,
Nuair a d'eitil tríd an gciúnas bán go míonla
  Spideog a bhí gan mhearbhall gan scáth:

Agus d'fhan os cionn na huaighe fé mar go mb'eol di
  Go raibh an toisc a thug í ceilte ar chách
Ach an té a bhí ag feitheamh ins an gcomhrainn,
  Is do rinneas éad fén gcaidreamh neamhghnách.

Do thuirling aer na bhFlaitheas ar an uaigh sin,
  Bhí meidhir uafásach naofa ar an éan,
Bhíos deighilte amach ón diamhairghnó im thuata
  Is an uaigh sin os mo chomhair in imigéin.

Le cumhracht bróin do folcadh m'anam drúiseach,
  Thit sneachta geanmnaíochta ar mo chroí,
Anois adhlacfad sa chroí a deineadh ionraic
  Cuimhne na mná d'iompair mé trí ráithe ina broinn.


The brightness of a young girl on her first communion day, the
brightness of the host on a Sunday altar, the brightness of milk squirt-
ing, escaping from the paps. When they buried my mother, brightness
of the sod.

My mind was scourging itself trying to fully taste the burial, when,
gently through the white silence, a robin flew without confusion or fear.

And she stayed above the grave as if she knew the reason that brought
her was hidden from all but the person waiting in the coffin, and I was
jealous of the extraordinary intimacy.

The air of Heaven descended on that grave, there was a terrible
saintly gaiety about the bird. A layman, I was kept apart from the
mysterious business; the grave before me in the distance.

My lustful soul was bathed with the fragrance of sorrow, a snow of
chastity fell on my heart. Now I will bury in the heart made upright the
memory of the woman who carried me nine months in her womb.

Tháinig na scológa le borbthorann sluasad,
    Is do scuabadar le fuinneamh an chré isteach san uaigh,
D'fhéachas-sa treo eile, bhí comharsa ag glanadh a ghlúine,
    D'fhéachas ar an sagart is bhí saoltacht ina ghnúis.

Grian an Mheithimh in úllghort,
    Is siosarnach i síoda an tráthnóna,
Beach mhallaithe ag portaireacht
    Mar screadstracadh ar an nóinbhrat.

Ranna beaga bacacha á scríobh agam,
    Ba mhaith liom breith ar eireaball spideoige,
Ba mhaith liom sprid lucht glanta glún a dhíbirt,
    Ba mhaith liom triall go deireadh lae go brónach.


## CLAUSTROPHOBIA

In aice an fhíona
Tá coinneal is sceon,
Tá dealbh mo Thiarna
D'réir dealraimh gan chomhacht,
Tá a dtiocfaidh den oíche
Mar shluaite sa chlós,


The gravediggers came with the violent noise of shovels and they vigorously swept the earth into the grave. I looked the other way, a neighbour was wiping his knee. I looked at the priest, there was worldliness in his face.

June sun in an orchard, a rustle in the silk of evening, an ill-tempered bee droning like a scream renting the evening-cloth.

I'm writing small halting verses, I'd like to catch hold of a robin's tail, I'd like to banish the spirit of knee-wipers. I'd like to journey sadly to the end of day.

*Claustrophobia*

Beside the wine there's a candle and terror, the statue of my Lord appears to be powerless. What will come of the night is like a crowd in

Tá rialtas na hoíche
Lasmuigh den bhfuinneoig;
Má mhúchann mo choinneal
Ar ball de m'ainneoin
Léimfidh an oíche
Isteach im scamhóig,
Sárófar m'intinn
Is ceapfar dom sceon,
Déanfar díom oíche,
Bead im dhoircheacht bheo:
    Ach má mhaireann mo choinneal
    Aon oíche amháin
    Bead im phoblacht solais
    Go dtiocfaidh an lá.


## REO


Maidin sheaca ghabhas amach
Is bhí seál póca romham ar sceach,
Rugas air le cur im phóca
Ach sciorr sé uaim mar bhí sé reoite:
Ní héadach beo a léim óm ghlaic
Ach rud fuair bás aréir ar sceach:


the yard, the government of night is outside the window. If my candle is quenched later in spite of me, the night will leap into my lung; my mind will be taken over and terror will be made for me. A night will be made of me, I will be a living darkness. But if my candle survives one night, I will be a republic of light until day comes.

*Freeze*

One frosty morning I roved out and a handkerchief was before me on a bush. I took it to put in my pocket but it slipped from me because it was frozen. It wasn't a living cloth that slipped from my grasp but a thing

Is siúd ag taighde mé fé m'intinn
Go bhfuaireas macasamhail an ní seo—
    Lá dar phógas bean dem mhuintir
    Is í ina cónra reoite, sínte.


## CNOC MELLERÍ

Sranntarnach na stoirme i Mellerí aréir
Is laethanta an pheaca bhoig mar bhreoiteacht ar mo
    chuimhne,
Laethanta ba leapacha de shonaschlúmh an tsaoil
Is dreancaidí na drúise iontu ag preabarnaigh ina mílte.

D'éirigh san oíche sidhe gaoithe coiscéim,
Manaigh ag triall ar an Aifreann,
Meidhir, casadh timpeall is rince san aer,
Bróga na manach ag cantaireacht.

Bráthair sa phroinnteach ag riaradh suipéir,
Tost bog ba bhalsam don intinn,
Ainnise naofa in oscailt a bhéil,
Iompar mothaolach Críostaí mhaith.


that died last night on a bush. And there I went searching in my mind
until I found an equivalent for this event—a day I kissed a woman of my
people when she lay in her coffin frozen.

*Mount Melleray*

The snoring of the storm in Melleray last night, and days of soft sin
like sickness on my memory, days that were beds of life's downy
contentment where the fleas of lust leaped by the thousands.
    A fairy-wind of footsteps rose in the night, monks on their way to
Mass, merriment, twirling and dancing in the air, the monks' shoes
chanting.
    A brother in the refectory preparing supper, soft silence was balsam
for the mind, a saintly misery in the opening of his mouth, the guileless
conduct of a good Christian.

Do doirteadh steall anchruthach gréine go mall
Trí mhúnla cruiceogach fuinneoige,
Do ghaibh sí cruth manaigh ó bhaitheas go bonn
Is do thosnaigh an ghrian ag léitheoireacht.

Leabhar ag an manach bán namhdach á léamh,
Go hobann casachtach an chloig,
Do múchadh an manach bhí déanta de ghréin
Is do scoilteadh an focal 'na phloic.

Buaileadh clog Complin is bhrostaigh gach aoi
Maolchluasach i dtreo an tséipéil;
Bhí beatha na naomh seo chomh bán le braitlín
Is sinne chomh dubh leis an daol.

Allas ar phaidrín brúite im láimh,
Mo bhríste dlúth-tháite lem ghlúin,
Ghluais sochraid chochallach manach thar bráid,
Ba shuarach leat féachaint a thabhairt.

Ach d'fhéachas go fiosrach gan taise gan trua
Mar fhéachadar Giúdaigh fadó
Ar Lazarus cúthail ag triall as an uaigh
Is géire na súl thart á dhó.


A formless splash of sunlight was spilt slowly through the lancet window, it took the shape of a monk from head to foot and the sun began to read.

A book being read by the white, hostile monk. Suddenly, the coughing of the bell, the monk made of sunlight was extinguished and the words in his cheeks were split.

The bell rang for Compline and all the guests hurried sheepishly towards the chapel, these saints' lives were white as a sheet and ourselves as black as a beetle.

Sweat on the rosary pressed in my hand, my trousers firmly stuck to my knee, a cowled procession of monks moved past, you'd think to look at them would be mean.

But I looked enquiringly without pity or compassion, as the Jews looked long ago on shy Lazarus coming from the grave, the sharpness of the eyes around burning him.

Do thiteadar tharainn 'na nduine is 'na nduine,
Reilig ag síorphaidreoireacht,
Is do thuirling tiubhscamall de chlúimh liath na cille
Go brónach ar ghrua an tráthnóna.

"Tá an bás ag cur seaca ar bheatha anseo,
Aige tá na manaigh ar aimsir,
Eisean an tAb ar a ndeineann siad rud,
Ar a shon deinid troscadh is treadhanas.

"Buachaill mar sheanduine meirtneach ag siúl,
Masla ar choimirce Dé,
An té 'dhéanfadh éagóir dá leithéid ar gharsún
Do chuirfeadh sé cochall ar ghréin;

"Do scaipfeadh an oíche ar fud an mheán lae,
Do bhainfeadh an teanga den abhainn,
Do chuirfeadh coir drúise in intinn na n-éan
Is do líonfadh le náire an domhan.

"Tá an buachaill seo dall ar an aigne fhiain
A thoirchíonn smaointe éagsúla
Gan bacadh le hAb ná le clog ná le riail
Ach luí síos le smaoineamh a dhúile.

They went past one by one, a graveyard incessantly praying, and a
dense cloud of the church's green mould fell sadly on the evening's
cheek.
"Death puts a frost over life here, the monks are his servants, he is the
abbot they serve, on whose behalf they fast and abstain.
"A boy walking like a weary old man, an insult to God's protection,
whoever would do such injustice to a boy would put a cowl over the sun.
"Would spread night over midday, would take the tongue from the
river, would place a crime of lust in the birds' minds and fill the world
with shame.
"This boy is blind to the lively mind that fertilises various thoughts,
without care for abbot or bell or rule but to lie down mulling over its
desire.

"Ní bhlaisfidh sé choíche tréanmheisce mná
A chorraíonn mar chreideamh na sléibhte,
'Thug léargas do Dante ar Fhlaitheas Dé tráth,
Nuair a thuirling na haingil i riocht véarsaí,"

Sin é dúirt an ego bhí uaibhreach easumhal,
Is é dallta le feirg an tsaoil,
Ach do smaoiníos ar ball, is an ceol os ár gcionn,
Gur mó ná an duine an tréad.

D'fhéachas laistiar díom ar fhásach mo shaoil,
Is an paidrín brúite im dhóid,
Peaca, díomhaointeas is caiteachas claon,
Blianta urghránna neantóg.

D'fhéachas ar bheatha na manach anonn,
D'aithníos dán ar an dtoirt,
Meadaracht, glaine, doimhinbhrí is comhfhuaim,
Bhí m'aigne cromtha le ceist.

Do bhlaiseas mórfhuascailt na faoistine ar maidin,
Aiseag is ualach ar ceal,
Scaoileadh an t-ancaire, rinceas sa Laidin,
Ba dhóbair dom tuirling ar Neamh.


"He will never taste the strong headiness of woman that moves mountains like faith, that once gave Dante a vision of Paradise when angels descended in the form of verses."

So spoke the ego, haughty and proud, blind with life's anger. But I thought later on, when the music was hanging over us, the flock is greater than the person.

I looked back at the desert of my life, the rosary squeezed in my hand, sin, sloth, misspent energy, hateful nettle-years.

I looked at the life of the monk over there, I immediately grasped a poem, metre, clarity, depth of meaning, alliteration, my mind was bent with anxiety.

I tasted the great release of confession this morning, restoration, a weight laid aside. The anchor was released, I danced in Latin, I almost landed in Heaven.

Ach do bhlaiseas, uair eile, iontaoibh asam féin,
Mo chuid fola ar fiuchadh le neart,
Do shamhlaíos gur lonnaigh im intinn Spiorad Naomh
Is gur thiteadar m'fhocail ó Neamh.

Buarach ar m'aigne Eaglais Dé,
Ar shagart do ghlaofainn coillteán,
Béalchráifeacht an Creideamh, ól gloine gan léan,
Mairfeam go dtiocfaidh an bás!

Manaigh mar bheachaibh ag fuaimint im cheann,
M'aigne cromtha le ceist,
Nótaí ag rothaíocht anonn is anall,
Deireadh le Complin de gheit.

Sranntarnach na stoirme i Mellerí aréir
Is laethanta an pheaca bhoig mar bhreoiteacht ar mo chuimhne
Is na laethanta a leanfaidh iad fá cheilt i ndorn Dé,
Ach greim fhir bháite ar Mhellerí an súgán seo filíochta.

But another time I tasted trust in myself, my blood boiling with
strength, I imagined the Holy Spirit settled in my mind and my words
falling from Heaven.

God's church was a spancel on my mind, I would call the priest a
eunuch, the faith hypocrisy; drink a glass without grief, let's live until
death comes!

Monks like bees murmuring in my head, my head bowed with
anxiety, notes wheeling hither and thither, Compline suddenly over.

The snoring of the storm in Melleray last night, and days of soft sin
like sickness on my memory, and the days that will follow them hidden
in God's fist, but this straw-rope of poetry is a drowning man's grip on
Melleray.

## CÚL AN TÍ

Tá Tír na nÓg ar chúl an tí,
    Tír álainn trína chéile,
Lucht ceithre chos ag siúl na slí
    Gan bróga orthu ná léine,
    Gan Béarla acu ná Gaeilge.

Ach fásann clóca ar gach droim
    Sa tír seo trína chéile,
Is labhartar teanga ar chúl an tí
    Nár thuig aon fhear ach Aesop,
    Is tá sé siúd sa chré anois.

Tá cearca ann is ál sicín,
    Is lacha righin mhothaolach,
Is gadhar mór dubh mar namhaid sa tír
    Ag drannadh le gach éinne,
    Is cat ag crú na gréine.

Sa chúinne thiar tá banc dramhaíl'
    Is iontaisí an tsaoil ann,
Coinnleoir, búclaí, seanhata tuí,
    Is trúmpa balbh néata,
    Is citeal bán mar ghé ann.

*Behind the House*

The Land of Youth's behind the house, a beautiful mixed-up land, four-footed ones walking the way without shoe or shirt, without English or Irish.

But in this higgledy-piggledy land a cloak grows on every back, and a language is spoken behind the house that no one understood but Aesop, and he is under the clay now.

There are hens there and a clutch of chickens; a steady clueless duck and a big black hound like an enemy in the land snarling at everyone, and a cat milking the sun.

In the far corner there's a rubbish heap with the wonders of the world there: candlesticks, buckles, an old straw hat; a neat dumb Jew's harp and a white kettle like a goose there.

Is ann a thagann tincéirí
    Go naofa, trína chéile,
Tá gaol acu le cúl an tí,
    Is bíd ag iarraidh déirce
    Ar chúl gach tí in Éirinn.

Ba mhaith liom bheith ar chúl an tí
    Sa doircheacht go déanach
Go bhfeicinn ann ar chuairt gealaí
    An t-ollaimhín sin Aesop
    Is é ina phúca léannta.

## FIABHRAS

Tá sléibhte na leapa mós ard,
Tá breoiteacht 'na brothall 'na lár,
Is fada an t-aistear urlár,
    Is na mílte is na mílte i gcéin
    Tá suí agus seasamh sa saol.

Atáimid i gceantar bráillín,
Ar éigean más cuimhin linn cathaoir,
    Ach bhí tráth sar ba mhachaire sinn,
    In aimsir choisíochta fadó,
    Go mbímis chomh hard le fuinneog.

It's there tinkers come, saintly, pell-mell. They are related to the back of the house and they beg behind every house in Ireland.

I'd like to be behind the house late in the darkness to see little Professor Aesop on a moonlight visit, and he a learned pooka.

*Fever*

The mountains of the bed are rather high and sickness a heat in there, the floor a long journey, and miles, miles away, life's sittings and standings go on.

We are in a place of sheets, we barely remember a chair. There was a time before we were a plain, in walking-times long ago, that we were tall as a window.

Tá pictiúir ar an bhfalla ag at,
Tá an fráma imithe ina lacht,
Ceal creidimh ní féidir é bhac,
        Tá nithe ag druidim fém dhéin,
        Is braithim ag titim an saol.

Tá ceantar ag taisteal ón spéir,
Tá comharsanacht suite ar mo mhéar,
Dob fhuirist dom breith ar shéipéal,
        Tá ba ar an mbóthar ó thuaidh,
        Is níl ba na síoraíochta chomh ciúin.


## NA LEAMHAIN


Fuaim ag leamhan leochaileach, iompó leathanaigh,
Bascadh mionsciathán,
Oíche fhómhair i seomra na leapa, tá
Rud leochaileach á chrá.

Oíche eile i dtaibhreamh bhraitheas-sa
Peidhre leamhan-sciathán,
Mar sciatháin aingil iad le fairsingeacht
Is bhíodar leochaileach mar mhná.


A picture swells on the wall, the frame has turned into liquid. Lacking faith we cannot stop it, things are moving towards me and I feel the world falling.

A place is travelling from the sky, a neighbourhood is settled on my finger, I could easily catch hold of a church. There are cows on the road to the North and the cows of eternity aren't as quiet.

*The Moths*

Sound of a fragile moth, turning of a page, bruising of small wings, an autumn night in the bedroom, a fragile thing is being tormented.

Another night in a dream I felt a pair of moth-wings. They were ample as an angel's wings, fragile as women.

Dob é mo chúram lámh a leagadh orthu
Is gan ligean leo chun fáin,
Ach iad a shealbhú gan sárú tearmainn
Is iad a thabhairt chun aoibhnis iomlán.

Ach dhoirteas-sa an púdar beannaithe
'Bhí spréite ar gach sciathán,
Is tuigeadh dom go rabhas gan uimhreacha,
Gan uimhreacha na fearúlachta go brách.

Is shiúil na deich n-uimhreacha as an mearbhall
Is ba mhó ná riamh a n-údarás,
Is ba chlos ciníocha ag plé le huimhreacha,
Is cách ba chlos ach mise amháin.

Fuaim ag leamhan leochaileach, iompó leathanaigh,
Creachadh leamhan-scannán,
Oíche fhómhair is na leamhain ag eiteallaigh
Mór mo bheann ar a mion-rírá.

It was my duty to touch them and not to let them go away, but to possess them without violating sanctuary and to bring them to full delight.

But I spilt the blessed powder that was spread on every wing and I realised I was without numbers, without the numbers of virility forever.

The ten numbers walked out of the confusion and their authority was greater than ever. And races were heard considering numbers and everyone was heard but me alone.

Sound of a fragile moth, turning of a page, ruining of the moth-film. Autumn night and the moths fluttering, I'm preoccupied with their minor uproar.

# Seán Ó Tuama

b. 1926

## CÁ SIÚLFAM?

Cá siúlfam? Tá na cosáin reoite,
carnáin chalcaithe de shneachta cruaite
ar bhlaincéadaí an bhóthair mar a mbíodh ár siúl.
'S tá an ghaoth ag aimsiú ioscada na nglún
chomh géar chomh glic le fuip. . . .
Ní shiúlfad leat. Tá an corp ina chloch.

Tiomáinfeam? Racham ar an aifreann déanach
ag éisteacht le Hosanna in Excelsis
á ghreadadh amach go buach caithréimeach,
is bainfeam sásamh as an at gan éifeacht
a thagann ar an gcroí. . . .
Chauffeur mé, lá seaca, ar dheabhóidí.

Ar deireadh: ní chorródsa amach inniu,
tá fuil i gcúl mo bhéil le mí ón sioc,
is ó inchinn go talamh síos
tá bánú déanta ar gach artaire
a dhéanann duine den daonaí. . . .
Fanfam féach an bhfillfidh teas arís.

## WHERE SHALL WE WALK?

Where shall we walk? The paths are all iced over,
On the grassy blankets of the roads we've known
Calcified mounds of slush and snow,
The wind stings the hollows of the knees
As slyly and as sharply as a whip. . . .
I shall not walk with you. The flesh is stone.

We shall drive then, go to Mass,
Listen to *Hosanna in Excelsis*
Being ground out triumphally,
And feed upon the silly satisfaction
Of music swelling up the heart. . . .
On a frosty day I act as chauffeur to the mysteries.

No, just no: I will not move today;
The chill has bloodied up my throat this long month past,
And every artery that makes a human burn
From brain down to the ground
Has been whitened to debility. . . .
We'll wait and see if heat returns.

## ROUSSEAU NA GAELTACHTA

Lig di, adúirt an file,
is ná smachtaigh í,
níl inti seo ach gearrchaile
is is breoiteacht é an t-eagla
a chrapann an nádúr.

Lig di, adúirt an file,
is ná smachtaigh í,
lig di fás gan bac ar bith
go dtína haoirde cheapaithe,
tá an t-aer fós bog os a cionn.


## "BESIDES, WHO KNOWS BEFORE THE END WHAT LIGHT MAY SHINE"

Maidin ghorm ins an Ghréig
(an leathchéad scoite agam)
faoi bhíomaí buí is giolcaigh fhite—
mo chorp ar teitheadh ón ngréin.

Liszt go glinn im chluais ag cumasc
le lapaíl shámh na dtonn,
táim síoraí anseo sa bhfuarthan
idir fallaí bána an tí.

An túisce stopann an pianó
tránn an mhuir fém chroí,
is cuimhním ar dhaoine age baile
a bhí mór im chathair tráth.

## A GAELTACHT ROUSSEAU

Let her be, said the poet;
do not chastise her,
she is still a stripling
and fear is a sickness
that stunts all human growth.

Let her be, said the poet;
do not chastise her,
let her grow unimpeded
to whatever height she is meant for:
the air is still soft above her head.

## "BESIDES, WHO KNOWS BEFORE THE END WHAT LIGHT MAY SHINE"

A blue mid-morning here in Greece
(my fiftieth year passed by),
under mottled beams and woven reeds—
body flees from sun.

Liszt, lucid in my ears, is merging
with the soft lap of the waves,
I'm immortal in this coolness,
enclosed between white walls.

As soon as the piano ceases
the sea ebbs from my heart
and I think of people home in my city
who, not long ago, stood high.

Ceathrar fear im chathairse
a éiríonn romham sa tost,
an luisne ard do mhúscail siad
do dheineas cimilt léi.

An saoi a chrith le gile an tsolais
i gceartain seanfhilí,
an draoi scaoil caisí ceoil thar cora—
is a bháigh é féin sa tsruth.

An file cráite a mhúnlaigh nua—
scamhóga Gaeilge dúinn,
an dealbhadóir chuir clocha ag rince
lena sheanchaíocht.

File, ceoltóir, dealbhadóir,
is rompu an máistir-saoi,
ina measc siúd do tharlaíos-sa;
ní tharlóidh sé arís.

Maidin ghorm ins an Ghréig
(an leathchéad scoite agam),
ag cuimhneamh ar an luisne a bhí—
is cúrsa é roimh bás.

Anois an t-am don rince aonair
ar ghainimh bheo na trá—
na cosa a chaitheamh go háiféiseach
is leá d'aonghnó sa teas.

Four men from my native city
rise before me now,
the glow of mind which they created
I rubbed against a while—:

a sage who trembled at the brightness
in the forge of ancient poets,
a druid who released our dammed-up music
and perished in the flood,

a tortured poet who fashioned for us
new Irish-language lungs,
a sculptor who set headstones dancing
with his carefree lore.

Musician, poet and sculptor,
and before them master-sage,
I happened to occur amongst them,
it will not occur again.

A blue mid-morning here in Greece
(my fiftieth year passed by)
thinking of the glow that was—
that's matter for the dying.

Better rise up now, a solo-dancer,
on the hot sands of the beach,
throw out both legs, at random,
and melt down in the sun.

## ISE SEACHTÓ HOCHT,
## EISEAN OCHTÓ CEATHAIR

Nuair pósadh iad adúramar
"Coinneoidh siad teas le chéile"
(ise caoga hocht, eisean seasca ceathair);
nuair cailleadh eisean, bhlaiseamar
an domlas 'nár mbéalaibh.

Ar dhéirc an stáit 'sea mhaireadar,
an tseanchaíocht a sólaist,—
ach bhí aghaidh seanrí ársa anois
ar chorp a fir sa tseomra.

Liúigh sí le fíoch, do chuardaigh é
le méireanna págánta,
is sinne go críostaí ag guí
go gcoiscfí an sruth bolcánach.

Is ba bhaintreach ise ó oirthear domhain,
seál dubh is beol féasógach,
an taon bhean riamh lem mharthainse
a thit i ngrá le prionsa
(ise seachtó hocht, eisean ochtó ceathair).

## SHE BEING 78, HE BEING 84

When they got married, we said
"They'll help to heat each other"
(she being 58, he being 64).
When he passed away we felt
bile rising in our mouths.

They had lived on dole and grants,
gossip their one solace—
but the dead face in the room now
was of an old king from the past.

She shrieked with rage, and combed him
with pagan fingerings
while we sound Christians prayed
that the lava-flow would stop.

She looked a widow of the Eastern world,
black shawl and moustached mouth,
the only woman in my lifetime
to have loved a prince
(she being 78, he being 84).

*translations by the author*

# Robert O'Donoghue

b. 1929

## DON JUAN

my autumn she might have been in the damp woods
all leaves falling:

it might have been between us the woods
when from fresh time we came walking in
and light on the lilacs in the room's corner
with anything we like playing from the radiogram
of tears and laughter in the large room of
imitations:

girlwoman with soot on her cheek—
it might have been a rug to sit on sipping
coffee I do not want
your book and mine open where we left them
a poem I read about the lily pond
and the tiger of love's eyes veiled:

but I fear the tinsel chivalry of this room
I feel and see what are the impulses and images
of madness in our tête-à-tête:

the heat of the logs I took from the damp woods
the protest from the scorched leaves
ask the several questions we will not answer.

my coat hangs in the hallway
soon the lights of a car will spotlight the landscape
the watchdogs will howl.

don't you see how much the fairytale depends
on the prince and the princess and the ogre.

what is it we might have been in the damp woods
all leaves falling.


## THE WITNESS


I had bare said matins
kissed the rood
when through the maingate
I saw them swarm

hundreds of the bastards:
some cunt, as always in Ireland,
had let them in.

Mary's son protect me
I burrowed into
the saltbarrel
farting copiously

as they ran past
the place of the women—
that would do for later—

heading for our crann beatha*
with their axes and knives
the hoors yelling like madmen

the tree in blossom
being hacked down by them
so it bled its red
petals over the earth.


*crann beatha: tree of life [ed.]

I was witness to that
I am witness to that today.

some boys threw themselves
on the warriors
on the veterans
were hacked down—

as you might expect—
it was hard to tell which
was blood and which petals.

the tree down
I knew my balls cut
all of our balls
and me a bard.

how would we function now?

with a split tongue
says Montague
as I lay in the barrel
shitting salt.

they took out the women then—
you never heard such squealing—
and mounted them in the courtyard.

Lord God be merciful
I was witness to that.

for seven centuries afterwards
I shat salt:
a severely debilitating disaster.

# Patrick Galvin

b. 1929


## LITTLE RED KNIFE

With my little red knife
I met my love
With my little red knife
I courted
And she stole me to her deep down bed
Her hair spread out a furnace red
But never a tender word was said
About my little red knife.

With my little red knife
I held her down
With my little red knife
I kissed her
And there in the sleep of her two blue eyes
I kissed and kissed a thousand lies
And opened wide her golden thighs
To please my little red knife.

With my little red knife
I made her weep
With my little red knife
I loved her
The wine was heavy in her mouth
The morning air stood up to shout
But there wasn't a living soul about
To see my little red knife.

With my little red knife
I raised her up
With my little red knife
I ripped her

And there in the gloom and rolling night
I cut her throat by candlelight
And hurried home to my waiting wife
Who damned my little red knife.


## PLAISIR D'AMOUR


### SPRING

My father
Against the victories of age
Would not concede defeat
He dyed his hair
And when my mother called
He said he wasn't there.

My mother, too
Fought back against the years
But in her Sunday prayers
Apologised to God.
My father said there was no God
"And that one knows it to her painted toes."

My mother smiled.
She'd plucked her eyebrows too
And wore a see-through skirt
With matching vest.
"He likes French knickers best" she said
"I'll have them blest."

My father raged.
He liked his women young, he said
And not half-dead.
He bought a second-hand guitar he couldn't play
And sang the only song he knew—
*Plaisir d'Amour.*

## SUMMER

When summer came
My father left the house
He tied a ribbon in his hair
And wore a Kaftan dress.
My mother watched him walking down the street
"He'll break his neck in that," she said—
"As if I care."

He toured the world
And met a guru in Tibet.
"I've slept with women too" he wrote
"And they not half my age."
My mother threw his letter in the fire—
"The lying ghett—he couldn't climb the stairs
With all his years."

She burned her bra
And wrote with lipstick on a card—
"I've got two sailors in the house
From Martinique.
They've got your children's eyes."
My father didn't wait to answer that
He came back home.

And sitting by the fire
He said he'd lied
He'd never slept with anyone but her.
My mother said she'd never lied herself—
She'd thrown the sailors out an hour before he came.
My father's heart would never be the same—
*Plaisir d'Amour.*


## AUTUMN

Through autumn days
My father felt the leaves
Burning in the corners of his mind.

My mother, who was younger by a year,
Looked young and fair.
The sailors from the port of Martinique
Had kissed her cheek.

He searched the house
And hidden in a trunk beneath the bed
My father found his second-hand guitar.
He found her see-through skirt
With matching vest.
"You wore French knickers once" he said
"I liked them best."

"I gave them all away," my mother cried
"To sailors and to captains of the sea.
I'm not half-dead
I'm fit for any bed—including yours."
She wore a sailor's cap
And danced around the room
While father strummed his second-hand guitar.

He made the bed
He wore his Kaftan dress
A ribbon in his hair.
"I'll play it one more time," he said
"And you can sing."
She sang the only song they knew—
*Plaisir d'Amour.*

WINTER

At sixty-four
My mother died
At sixty-five
My father.

Comment from a neighbour
Who was there:
"They'd pass for twenty."
*Plaisir d'Amour.*

## MISS CECILY FINCH

Miss Finch is dead.

In my day we lived south of the city
A large house, going cheap, and due for demolition.
In my day it was pleasant to live south of the city
And Miss Finch was forty years old.

Who was Miss Finch?
I wish I knew.

Her portrait hung upon the wall
In this house, going cheap, and due for demolition.
Her name printed underneath:
Miss Cecily Finch
My house—bought and paid for in hard cash.

Miss Cecily Finch
Had money in the bank.

The house she lived in had a yellow face
The bathroom painted green
The stairs purple like a Roman Mass.
A country lass?
The dying roses in the hall proclaimed her taste.

Miss Cecily Finch
Had found her place.

When we moved in we cleaned the rooms
And swept the roses from the petalled hall
The stairs we painted white, the bathroom red,
Miss Finch was dead.
Her portrait, heavy on the nail, we dragged to the basement.

The door locked
On Miss Cecily Finch.

A famine week
And Dublin at its greyest peak
Shed tears of anguish for Miss Cecily Finch
Damp in the basement and crying to come out
I heard her shout: My house
Bought and paid for in hard cash.

Miss Cecily Finch
Ripe for demolition.

We set her free
Returned her portrait to the crumbling wall
Saw green grow on the bathroom shelf
And purple cover the stairs.
The dying roses in the street came back to greet
Miss Cecily Finch.

Who was Miss Cecily Finch?
A special case?
Her portrait hangs upon the wall
And dares me shift it from her chosen place.


## THE BARD

It's a great curse to be living now
In this season of common poets.
Would that I were back in former times
When all poets were measured in learning.

Twelve years we spent in a school
Making the art of true poetry.
Look at them now walking the streets
Shabby in verse and bursting with ignorance.

Grandeur in dress and eloquent of speech
Renowned in virtue and adorned with sense
The poet gone by was more than welcome
In noble houses of respected lords.

With food provided and bed made ready
His name was honoured and his word was law—
But more than that, his poems were paid for
With three milch-cows and a barrel of ale.

A pox and blight on the common jobber
Who ruined the trade of decent poets.
I'll write no more and return to nature
Commune with horses and lie down with sheep.


## THE AUNT


On All Souls' Night
My father said the aunt was due.
We set a table near the fire
A glass of wine, a loaf of bread.
Was that the way to greet the dead?
My father said it was.

At three o'clock the aunt arrived
I heard her knocking at the door
And I went down to let her in.
Her eyes were wide and black as sloes
And she had clay upon her clothes
And she was thin.

Her breath was cold.
And as we sat beside the fire
I asked her if she'd like some wine.
She said she never touched the stuff
And honest bread was quite enough
When you were dead.

I watched her eating for an hour
And saw the grave beneath the skin
The moonlight through the bone.
Now and then she coughed and cried
And said she wished she hadn't died
The nights were chill.

At four o'clock she rose to go
But as she reached the kitchen door
She turned and kissed me on the lips
And then she smiled—
When you are not your father's child
We two shall wed.


## ADVICE TO A POET


Be a chauffeur, my father said
And never mind the poetry.
That's all very well for the rich
They can afford it.
What you need is money in your belt
Free uniform and plenty of travel.
Besides that, there's nothing in verse.
And all poets are raging homosexuals.

*I'd still like to be a poet.*

Another thing: don't ever marry
And if you do, then marry for cash.
Love, after all, is easily come by
And any old whore will dance for a pound.
Take my advice and be a chauffeur
The uniform will suit you a treat
Marriage and poems will blind you surely
And poets and lovers are doomed to hell.

*I'd still like to be a poet.*

But where's the sense in writing poetry?
Did any poet ever make good?
I never met one who wasn't a pauper
A prey to bailiffs, lawyers and priests.
Take my advice and be a chauffeur
With your appearance you're bound to do well
You might even meet some rich old widow
Who'll leave you a fortune the moment she dies.

*I'd still like to be a poet.*

Well, blast you then, your days are darkened
Poverty, misery, carnage and sin.
The poems you'll write won't be worth a penny.
And the women you marry will bleed you to death.
Take my advice and buy a revolver
Shoot yourself now in the back of the head.
The Government then might raise a subscription
To keep your poor father from breeding again.


## THE MADWOMAN OF CORK


*To-day*
*Is the feast day of Saint Anne*
*Pray for me*
*I am the madwoman of Cork.*

Yesterday
In Castle Street
I saw two goblins at my feet
I saw a horse without a head
Carrying the dead
To the graveyard
Near Turner's Cross.

*I am the madwoman of Cork*
*No one talks to me.*

When I walk in the rain
The children throw stones at me
Old men persecute me
And women close their doors.
When I die
Believe me
They'll set me on fire.

*I am the madwoman of Cork*
*I have no sense.*

Sometimes
With an eagle in my brain
I can see a train
Crashing at the station.
If I told people that
They'd choke me—
Then where would I be?

*I am the madwoman of Cork*
*The people hate me.*

When Canon Murphy died
I wept on his grave
That was twenty-five years ago.
When I saw him just now
In Dunbar Street
He had clay in his teeth
He blest me.

*I am the madwoman of Cork*
*The clergy pity me.*

I see death
In the branches of a tree
Birth in the feathers of a bird.
To see a child with one eye
Or a woman buried in ice

Is the worst thing
And cannot be imagined.

*I am the madwoman of Cork*
*My mind fills me.*

I should like to be young
To dress up in silk
And have nine children.
I'd like to have red lips
But I'm eighty years old
I have nothing
But a small house with no windows.

*I am the madwoman of Cork*
*Go away from me.*

And if I die now
Don't touch me.
I want to sail in a long boat
From here to Roche's Point
And there I will anoint the sea
With oil of alabaster.

*I am the madwoman of Cork*
*And to-day is the feast day of*
*Saint Anne.*
*Feed me.*

# MESSAGE TO THE EDITOR

Sir—
   The Lord pardon the people of this town
   Because I can't.
   When I dropped dead in the street
   Three weeks ago
   I thought they'd bury me in style.
   A state funeral was the least of it
   With Heads of Government and the Nobility
   In attendance.
   I even looked forward to the funeral oration
   In Irish
   With a few words on my past achievements:
   Our greatest poet, a seat in heaven to the man
   And how I deserved better.

   But did I get it?
   My corpse lay in Baggot Street
   For a fortnight
   Before anyone noticed it.
   And when I was finally removed
   To the mortuary
   I was abused by a medical student
   Who couldn't open a bag of chips
   Let alone the body of your greatest poet.
   Then, to add to the indignity
   I was pushed into an ice-box
   And some clod stuck a label on my foot
   Saying: unknown bard—probably foreign.

   If it wasn't
   For a drunken Corkman
   Who thought I was his dead brother
   I'd still be lying unclaimed.
   At least
   The man had the decency to bury me.
   But where am I?

Boxed in some common graveyard
Surrounded by peasants
And people of no background.
When I think of the poems I wrote
And the great prophecies I made
I could choke.

I can't write now
Because the coffin is too narrow
And there's no light.
I'm trying to send this
Through a medium
But you know what they're like—
Table-tapping bastards
Reeking of ectoplasm.
If you manage to receive this
I'd be glad if you'd print it.
There's no point in asking you
To send me a copy—
I don't even know my address.

# Seán Lucy

b. 1931


## LONGSHORE INTELLECTUAL

After all, Charlie, we shall see them go,
And feel renewal with the buff sails stirring,
After this bad weather the tall fleets will embark
Leaving the women on the quayside staring.

The dark pubs at night will become old men's places
Where the wind rattles the bar-room shutters:
Knowing only in retrospect the loud voices and beery faces,
Dim as the inarticulate story the senile drinker stutters.

And after all, Charlie, they are the men of action:
We chose the shore life of the seedy dreamer,
Deliberately abandoning the ships then weighing anchor,
Deliberately ignoring the bravado recruiting drummer.

It only needles us when they come home in glory
In cameraderie and the glow of doing,
Making their memory into a mutual and lovely story,
Leaving us wordless with our book contentment dying;

They steal our women and deride our wisdom,
They drink our whiskey and borrow our possessions,
This is their ancient and abiding custom,
With uncultured voices and unbridled passions.

But after all, Charlie, we know how they end:
Their bodies washing on the beaches of far nations,
Their eye sockets empty, their mouths full of sand,
And their girl-friends lonely—we have our consolations.

# DONAL OGUE

Donal Ogue, if you cross the water
Take me with you and don't forget to,
At fair and market you shall have a fairing
And the Greek King's daughter for your bed-companion.

If you go away I've a way to know you:
Two green eyes and the bright fair head of you,
A dozen curls on your top-knot clustering
Like a bright yellow flag or a rose in flowering.

And late last night the watchdog spoke of you,
The snipe declared you in the deepest bogland,
And you, all alone, gone through the woodlands . . .
And be lonely always until you marry me.

You made a promise, and you told a lie then,
To come and meet me where sheep are folded,
I whistled loud and I shouted often
With no reply but a small lamb bleating.

You made a promise, one of difficulty,
Ships of gold all rigged with silver,
A dozen towns, in each a market,
And a limewhite palace beside the seashore.

You made a promise, a thing unlikely,
That you would give me fine gloves of fishskin,
That you would give me fine shoes of birdskin,
And a suit of silk the dearest in Erin.

O Donal Ogue, I'd suit you better
Than a noble lady proud and haughty,
I'd milk the cow and I'd turn the churn for you,
And if things were difficult I'd strike a blow for you.

O my grief! And it's not the hunger,
The want of food, drink, or sleep enough

That has left me so thin and perishing,
But a young man's love that has surely wasted me.

At early morning I sighted my truelove
Up on horseback riding the roadway,
He passed me by and he didn't call me,
On returning home again I was crying sorely.

When by myself at the Well of Loneliness
Sitting down I make my sorrowing,
I see the world and no trace of my darling
With the glow of amber on his warm cheeks shining.

That was the Sunday I gave my love to you,
The very Sunday before Easter Sunday,
I was reading the Passion on my knees devoutly
And yet my eyes were sending love to you.

Mother said to me not to speak to you
Today nor tomorrow nor on the Sunday,
But bad the time she chose for telling me,
'Twas locking the door up after the robbery.

Mother, my little one, give me to him,
And also give to him all of your property,
Out yourself and beg for charity
And don't come East or West to find me.

My heart is black as a sloe inside me,
Or the blackest coal that's in the forge there,
Or a dark footprint in the gleaming hallways,
And 'twas you that turned my life so black and bitter.

You've taken East from me and you've taken West from me,
And what's before me and what's behind me,
You've taken sun from me and you've taken moon from me,
And my fear is terrible you've taken God from me.

*Anonymous, 18th–19th century*
*translated by Seán Lucy*

## *from* UNFINISHED SEQUENCE
## FOR SEÁN Ó RIADA

VII    HOMO LUDENS

And he told this story
of the old singer and the tape recorder:
of how the old man listened to his own voice
while fierce anxiety turned down his mouth
until he heard his strengthening voice
move into life again.
Then sat with concentration till the song was over,
flung his cap on the floor between his boots
crying,

     "I'll never die!"

Another night Seán sat down at the piano
when we were drinking poitín and pints of stout
and played that tune to me for the first time,
that air of pride and loss,
of the sharp love that has accepted loss.
And in his hands our deadly lasting sadness
became acceptable
so I was moved to tears;
not drunk but steady,
I cried,
and when he finished cursed him saying, "You bastard,
you took me by surprise."
He stood up with his fingers round my arm
smiling and laughing;
pleased with my understanding,
more pleased by his power,
most deeply pleased by music
    by the thing itself.

One afternoon he said,
"A man should dance on his own floor."

And he danced.

### VIII    NIGHTLIGHT

You'd never have called her pretty, but she was beautiful,
and shines still twenty years on and more,
and shines in his dead heart
maybe, because predictable and powerful
the love forcefield controls phenomena before
and after, cracking normal time apart;

which, in witnessing often, we have strange reasons for hope,
hope which some might take for despair
(different meanings for 'doom'):
as, when after his death, wondering how she could cope,
she said she often knew he was sitting awake reading
    somewhere
in an empty bed in an empty room.

He was frightened of dark, and sleep seemed to him like death;
so, if she stayed late at a party after he left,
he would sit up defiant with book and light,
paying the closest attention to doubtful pulse and breath,
until she came in shining alive
and made him warm in the cold night.

# Desmond O'Grady

b. 1935

## THE POET IN OLD AGE
## FISHING AT EVENING

*for Ezra Pound*

Comes a time
When even the old and familiar ideas
Float out of reach of the mind's hooks,
And the soul's prime
Has slipped like a fish through the once high weirs
Of an ailing confidence. O where are the books
On this kind of death?

Upright as love
Out on the tip of a tail of rock,
The sea ravelling off from the eye,
The line like the nerve
Straining the evening back from the clock,
He merges awhile into the lie
Of his own silhouette.


## SIGHTSEEING

In the centre, the ancient churchyard, a national
Monument, giving out on a view of the valley
Where thickening hay, with the breeze like smoke
On its surface, gleams in the light like the brushstroked
Coat of a fairhaired animal—the bevy
Of crosses inclined to be lackadaisical

Like the spearheads of guardsmen at ease.
Not far to the left on a once moated mound
The exploded remains of a castle in motion
But petrified now at the point of disintegration.
To the right and down lower ground,
Hidden by beeches, some minor remains

With Romanesque portals in good preservation.
Ahead, and over the tufted grass
And the flagstones, between the bundle of bone-
Like crosses, the tomb with an old boot thrown on its
    topstone—
A touch of mortality—the deep boss
Of the river curves with a darkening motion.

Then after inspecting the architecture,
The doors and the windows, the restoration;
After tracing our fingers over the outlines
Left on the panelled stone by weather and winds;
With a mumbled-on-leaving appreciation—
Mere repetition of previous conjecture

On the state of a fragment—we move to the railing
For the car and the thermos of afternoon tea,
The chocolate biscuit, the sliver of lemon.
With the ancient locality as still as a woman,
The river getting on with going to sea,
We sip, while the castle holds back from its falling.


*from* THE DARK EDGE OF EUROPE


A twist of cloth on the flat stones
Close by her heel in the rocky ford,
The peasant woman, bowed, unaware
Of the age on her back, the ache in her bones,
Washes away by the bend in the road
At the heel of the hill, a rag in her hair.

Farther behind in a yard full of haycocks
Her man and his son untackle the cart,
Stable the oxen, hang up the harness,
Their day done. One knocks
The crusted clay from the belly part
Of a shovel. The other stands in silence.

The valley suspends its diurnal labour.
Lake and island hang in the sky.
The sun, blocked by the broken wall
Of a castle, sinks with a stone's languor
Into the evening. The caught eye
Swivels to a hawk's impending fall.

By the butt of an ancient tree a boy,
My guide, squats sucking a stalk;
His head, his noble historical head,
Cocked like an animal's, his mind's eye
Fixed upon nothing. Out on the dark
Edge of Europe my love is dead.


## READING THE UNPUBLISHED MANUSCRIPTS OF LOUIS MACNEICE AT KINSALE HARBOUR

One surely tires eventually of the frequent references—
    the gossip
praise, the blame, the intimate anecdote—to those
who, for one unpredictable reason or other (living
abroad, difference of age, chance, the friends one chose,
being detained too long at the most opportune moment) one
never, face to tactile face, has met; but who
had the way things fall fallen favourably, once met, for some
right psychic force, would have been polar, kindred you—
though time, space, human nature, sometimes contract
to force the action done that makes abstraction fact.

Here in this mock of a room which might have been yours,
   might have been
the place of our eventual meeting, I find a berth temporarily
(so long too late) among your possessions. Alone,
except for your face in the framed photos,
I sit with your manuscripts spread over my knees,
reliving the unpublished truths of your autobiography.
On the shelves and table, desk, floor, your books
and papers, your bundles of letters—as if you were just
   moving in
or out, or had been already for years—
like a poem in the making you'll never now finish.
Through the windows I see down to the hook of
   Old Kinsale Harbour.
Mid-summer. Under the sun the sea as smooth as a dish.
Below on the quays the fishermen wind up the morning's
   business:
stacking the fishboxes, scraping the scales from their
   tackle and hands.
Behind this house the hills shovel down on the town's
   slate roofs
the mysterious green mounds of their history.
Flaming fir, clouted holly.
Not an Irish harbour at all, but some other—
the kind you might find along the Iberian coast, only greener.

Down to here, down to this clay of contact between us, Hugh
   O'Neill once marched
from way up your part of the country, the North, the winter
   of sixteen
hundred and one, to connect with the long needed Spaniards
   three months
under siege in the Harbour. Having played the English their
   own game and watched
all his life for his moment, he lost our right lot in one bungled
   night
and with it the thousands of years of our past and our future.
   He began

what divides the North they brought your ash back to, from the
    South I have left
for Rome—where O'Neill's buried exiled. And here, then, this
    moment, late
as the day is (what matter your physical absence) I grow
    towards your knowing,
towards the reassurance of life in mortality, the importance, the
    value of dying.


## PROFESSOR KELLEHER AND
## THE CHARLES RIVER

The Charles river reaps here like a sickle. April
Light sweeps flat as ice on the inner curve
Of the living water. Overhead, far from the wave, a dove-
White gull heads inland. The spring air, still
Lean from winter, thaws. Walking, John
Kelleher and I talk on the civic lawn.

West, to our left, past some trees, over the ivy walls,
The clock towers, pinnacles, the pillared university yard,
The Protestant past of Cambridge New England
    selfconsciously dead
In the thawing clay of the Old Burying Ground. Miles
East, over the godless Atlantic, our common brother,
Ploughing his myth-muddy fields, embodies our order.

But here, while the students row by eights and fours
    on the river—
As my father used to row on the Shannon when, still a child,
I'd cross Thomond Bridge every Sunday, my back
    to the walled
And turreted castle, listening to that uncle Mykie deliver
His version of history—I listen now to John Kelleher
Unravel the past a short generation later.

Down at the green bank's nerve ends, its roots half in the river,
A leafing tree gathers refuse. The secret force
Of the water worries away the live earth's under-surface.
But his words, for the moment, hold back time's being's
    destroyer,
While the falling wave on both thighs of the ocean
Erodes the coasts, at its dying conceptual motion.

Two men, one young, one old, stand stopped acrobats,
    in the blue
Day, their bitch river to heel. Beyond,
Some scraper, tower or ancestral house's gable end.
Then, helplessly, as in some ancient dance, the two
Begin their ageless struggle, while the tree's shadow
With all its arms, crawls on the offal-strewn meadow.

Locked in their mute struggle there by the blood-loosed tide
The two abjure all innocence, tear down past order—
The one calm, dispassionate, clearsighted; the other
Wild with ecstasy, intoxicated, world mad.
Surely some new order is at hand;
Some new form emerging where they stand.

Dusk. The great dim tide of shadows from the past
Gathers for the end—the living and the dead.
All force is fruitful. All opposing powers combine.
Aristocratic privilege, divine sanction, anarchy at last
Yield the new order. The saffron sun sets.
All shadows procession in an acropolis of lights.

# AFTERNOON

Afternoon, and the houses are quiet as dust at the foot of a wall.
The tea and the coffee things cleared away from the talk and
    the thinking,
The magazines flicked through, the telephone tempting, the
    sand in the hourglass sinking,
The waiting—knowing nothing will happen at all.

Afternoon, and just for the want of something more daring
    to do
Lunch is being seriously digested in the serious bowels
    of the town.
The buses are empty, the taxis unwanted and lorries are caught
    in a brown
Study of idleness. Business is slow.

In the parks and the playgrounds, shifty-eyed watchers in
    colourless clothes
Are hanging around like agents of death, while professional
    loungers,
In soft hats and silence, disinterestedly wait for the next
    observation; and scroungers
And tricksters are nervously watching what goes.

Down by the shipless, motionless docks; abandoned by all
Except for a stray indefinable blur of what must be a man
And the inevitable rake of a pigeon scratching for corn;
    the cranes
Are struck dead—unable even to fall.

The voice on the radio—remote, unmelodic—gives news
    of events
And things that are happening—urban expansion, rural
    improvements,
Revolutions and riots, social reforms and new intellectual
    movements—
In lands with more future than this one presents.

In the lanes and the archways the children are few, the lovers
    fewer still
And those who are left have plans and intentions of joining
    the rest
On emigrant tickets. In the streets there is no one but old men
    and widows, cursed
With sorry separation and a broken will.

Crack, and the shouts of men go up as a rat breaks cover
To die by the stones and the longhandled sticks of exasperation
Back of the wagons in the stopped yards of the black,
    uneventful station—
And just for a moment the waiting is over.


## THE OLD WAYS


We grew away from the old ways
familiar to us in childhood and fell
into a black circle of foreign habits.
We forgot the holy wells and places
where people gathered, without clearly
remembering the reason, on certain days; forgot
the old mysterious festivals for the different
seasons like fire-jumping on a summer hill;
ancient practices like blood-letting
on a new threshold and funeral games.
We said they were for superstitious old women
and we aped the ways of the foreigner.
Then we had nothing—neither a past
for precedent nor a future foreseeable.
With the old ways we had some idea
what the year held in store: with their help
we could face and endure it.
We knew a kind of visible security,
the security of a familiar ritual.
Without the old ways we became
loose straws in a black wind.
With what shall we now replace them?

*from* HELLAS

Here, because of the shock, the sudden
rage of our disappointment,
because brute thoroughness of execution
brought quick death, sorry wedding,
Greece and you have been in all our thoughts,
on all our tongues. Over morning coffee,
late over drinks into the radio-reporting
night—the daily newspapers scattered
like blasted doves about the room—
we have talked of your dark present,
your unforeseeable future, the past's example.
Even when alone in the street,
on a bus, reading, at work,
you and Greece have been raging in silent riot
through my head like the despaired history
of my own country.

That night, at Patrick Creagh's house,
Vasilikos, stranded, arrived with his woman.
Three men with our women, our several
pasts, fragmented emotions, we imagined
the same hour in Athens shocked
groups, watching and watched, sat
behind barred windows, bolted doors,
like Jews in a ghetto.
Vasilikos, his name on the list of arrests
in *Le Monde*, talked Greece and her past
in postmortem and Patrick and I
spoke her poems out loud, turn
around, like a requiem.

There in that house of so many unspoken
remembrances (that one day we can all
share for a brief, intense while)
the spirits of Greece, living and dead,
were amongst and around us: Cavafis,

Elytis, Aeschylus, Archilochus,
Amphis and Gatsos, Menander, Sophocles,
Socrates, Plato, Seferis and Ritsos . . .
And our thoughts! Our thoughts!

Afterwards, going home through the dark
to the late night news—
the shock, like a death or final
departure, still harder than marble
or honour back of the eyeballs—
an old song came into my head
from my own country:
Mise Éire
'Sine mé ná an Cailleach Béara
Mór mo ghlór
Mé do rug Cuchullain crógach
Mór mo náir
Mo chlann féin do dhíol a mháthair
Mise Éire
Uaigneach mé ná an Cailleach Béara:—
I am Ireland
I am older than the Hag of Beare Island
Great my pride
I mothered brave Cuchulain
Great my shame
My own family sold their mother
I am Ireland
I am lonelier than the Hag of Beare Island.

# Brendan Kennelly

b. 1936

## THE GIFT

It came slowly.
Afraid of insufficient self-content
Or some inherent weakness in itself
Small and hesitant
Like children at the tops of stairs
It came through shops, rooms, temples,
Streets, places that were badly-lit,
It was a gift that took me unawares
And I accepted it.

## BLACKBIRD

This shiny forager cocks his head
As if listening for the sound
Of killable phenomena
Underground.

He depends entirely
On the sharp eye and ear,
On the ravening stab
Of a yellow beak

From which just now,
Spontaneous as light, pure as flame,
Impassioning the chill day,
Such music came

I scarce believe his murderous competence
As he stabs to stay alive,
Choking music
That music may survive.


## THE SWIMMER

For him the Shannon opens
Like a woman.
He has stepped over the stones

And cut the water
With his body;
But this river does not bleed for

Any man. How easily
He mounts the waves, riding them
As though they

Whispered subtle invitations to his skin,
Conspiring with the sun
To offer him

A white, wet rhythm. The deep beneath
Gives full support
To the marriage of wave and heart.

The waves he breaks turn back to stare
At the repeated ceremony
And the hills of Clare

Witness the fluent weddings,
The flawless congregation,
The choiring foam that sings

To limbs which must, once more,
Rising and falling in the sun,
Return to shore.

Again he walks upon the stones,
A new music in his heart,
A river in his bones

Flowing forever through his head
Private as a grave
Or as the bridal bed.


## THE TIPPLER

Out of the clean bones
He tipples a hard music.
Cocking his head,
He knows himself sole master of his trade.
Hence his pride.

A goat ran wild
Through field and hillside,
Was tracked, caught, tethered, tamed,
Butchered and no man cried.
And the Tippler got his bones.

All bones dry in the sun,
Harden to browny white,
Mere flesh stripped and gone;
But bones create a new delight
When clacked by the proper man.

Let flesh lie rotten
When the Tippler takes his stand,
Holds the bones between his fingers;
Death has given him command,
Permitted him his hunger,

Made his heart articulate,
Tender, proud,
Clacking at shoulder, chest and head.
That man is for a while unbowed
Who brings music from the dead.


## MY DARK FATHERS

My dark fathers lived the intolerable day
Committed always to the night of wrong,
Stiffened at the hearthstone, the woman lay,
Perished feet nailed to her man's breastbone.
Grim houses beckoned in the swelling gloom
Of Munster fields where the Atlantic night
Fettered the child within the pit of doom,
And everywhere a going down of light.

And yet upon the sandy Kerry shore
The woman once had danced at ebbing tide
Because she loved flute music—and still more
Because a lady wondered at the pride
Of one so humble. That was long before
The green plant withered by an evil chance;
When winds of hunger howled at every door
She heard the music dwindle and forgot the dance.

Such mercy as the wolf receives was hers
Whose dance became a rhythm in a grave,
Achieved beneath the thorny savage furze
That yellowed fiercely in a mountain cave.
Immune to pity, she, whose crime was love,
Crouched, shivered, searched the threatening sky,
Discovered ready signs, compelled to move
Her to her innocent appalling cry.

Skeletoned in darkness, my dark fathers lay
Unknown, and could not understand

The giant grief that trampled night and day,
The awful absence moping through the land.
Upon the headland, the encroaching sea
Left sand that hardened after tides of Spring,
No dancing feet disturbed its symmetry
And those who loved good music ceased to sing.

Since every moment of the clock
Accumulates to form a final name,
Since I am come of Kerry clay and rock,
I celebrate the darkness and the shame
That could compel a man to turn his face
Against the wall, withdrawn from light so strong
And undeceiving, spancelled in a place
Of unapplauding hands and broken song.


## BREAD


Someone else cut off my head
In a golden field.
Now I am re-created

By her fingers. This
Moulding is more delicate
Than a first kiss,

More deliberate than her own
Rising up
And lying down.

Even at my weakest, I am
Finer than anything
In this legendary garden

Yet I am nothing till
She runs her fingers through me
And shapes me with her skill.

The form that I shall bear
Grows round and white.
It seems I comfort her

Even as she slits my face
And stabs my chest.
Her feeling for perfection is

Absolute.
So I am glad to go through fire
And come out

Shaped like her dream.
In my way
I am all that can happen to men.
I came to life at her fingerends.
I will go back into her again.


## A KIND OF TRUST

I am happy now.
You rose from your sick bed
After three weeks. Your heart was low

When the world grew small,
A white ceiling
And four yellow walls.

Let me say again what this means
To me. As far as I know
Love always begins

Like a white morning
Of seagulls near the window,
Messengers bringing

Word that we must up and out
Into a small garden
Where there are late

Apples we shall find
So ripe that the slightest touch
Will pitch them to the ground.

Best things seem content to fall and fail.
I am not good enough for that.
I fight the drag and pull

Of any kind of dying
And bitterly insist
On that white morning

When you weakly climb the stairs,
Letting new life reach you like a gift
There at the brown bannister.

I do not insist
Out of panic or vague dread
But out of a kind of trust

In this beginning
With late apples and early seagulls
And a young sun shining

When you let cold water flow into a cup,
Steady yourself between two chairs
And stand straight up.

## WE ARE LIVING

What is this room
But the moments we have lived in it?
When all due has been paid
To gods of wood and stone
And recognition has been made
Of those who'll breathe here when we are gone,
Does it not take its worth from us
Who made it because we were here?

Your words are the only furniture I can remember,
Your body the book that told me most.
If this room has a ghost
It will be your laughter in the frank dark,
Revealing the world as a room
Loved only for those moments when
We touched the purely human.

I could give water now to thirsty plants,
Dig up the floorboards, the foundation,
Study the worm's confidence,
Challenge his omnipotence
Because my blind eyes have seen through walls
That make safe prisons of the days.

We are living
In ceiling, floor and windows,
We are given to where we have been.
This white door will always open
On what our hands have touched,
Our eyes have seen.

# Michael Coady

b. 1939

## SECOND HONEYMOON

This old dowager must be
plugged, sealed and painted
before her coming out.

Scraper and wire brush
bare mercilessly
her private decay.

Talk
is all of boats,
rightly seasoned wood
and great years for fish.

Three boards need major surgery—
new wood measured,
cut and planed,
snugged in with copper rivets.

Newspaper, caulking-twine and putty
seal up her rent joints and cavities.

Three coats of tar then
clothe her multitude of sins.

On a high June tide
we ease her through the reeds.

Her lover greets her, trickling
and probing through the boards
until she swells.

In the half-light
she still has girlish grace—

sea-lice and salmon-scales and blood
she'll know again.


## TWO FOR A WOMAN, THREE FOR A MAN

The bell hangs eighty feet
above the town
in a granite tower
raised on sweated pennies of the poor
after Emancipation.

Familiar as domestic air or sky
the resonant summons to Mass or Angelus
measures in stale ritual
each ordinary day;
we almost don't hear
but notice something missing
when once a year
the death of Christ
strikes the iron dumb
for two whole days
until Easter stirs the grave-cloths
and frees the frozen tongue
to sound out joy.

Throughout the wider circle of the year
the bell tolls for each human death
and people in pubs and shops,
standing on the street
or leaning on the bridge
raise their heads
and count the strokes:
two for a woman,
three for a man—

The knell proclaims reprieve:
*Who's dead?* is edged
with self-congratulation.

When the bell boomed three
over my father's coffin
my emigrant brother pale
above his black tie shuddered
*I couldn't live
under that sound.*

I could have said that though
there are other places
there are other bells
and there is no
emancipation.

In evening silhouette
a great spider hangs
above this town of some
five thousand souls.

Each of us moves
on a gossamer thread
mortally tethered
to its patient web.


## OH NO, 'TWAS THE TRUTH

The girl sipped her fourth vodka and said
She found people in general boring—
Then she smiled and added that this was not true
Of the man she was with at the moment.

"I'm flattered," I said, "though I can't quite agree
With that proposition."
Her lips were moist and the front of her blouse
Was straining towards fruition.

A man at the bar unsheathed his voice
And impaled *The Rose of Tralee*,
The girl grimaced, leaned forward and spoke
With tipsy intensity.

"I suppose my mind is starved," she said,
"For want of good company,
I often talk to myself—I suspect
My friends think I'm a bit queer."

"Hold on a moment," I interposed,
"You verge there on the metaphysical:
*I* talk to *myself*—that makes you two
In plain and simple addition

And there's also the you that observes the I
That talks to the self, which makes three—
Though to tell you the truth I wouldn't object
If you stretched to infinity."

*The Rose of Tralee* was close to a climax
In the nose of the man at the bar,
She was lovely and fair like the rose of the summer
And her lips were close to my ear.

"The truth is I have lots of selves
But which of them is me?
I wonder sometimes who I am
Or what I'm meant to be."

"Ah there's the thing we must tease out
Before this night is done,
Given congenial company
Metaphysics can be fun

As long as you never hide behind
That neutered English form—
'One strays with one's love to the pure crystal fountain . . .'
Who the hell is this One?"

*The Rose* was trembling on the air,
She laughed, pink tongue, white teeth,
"It's so refreshing to talk like this
But God it's noisy here!"

I said I had a quiet room
Where One never darkened the door;
We took a bottle and left to pursue
The metaphysics of self once more.

Alone together we uncorked truth
And with each sip of wine
The prefix in metaphysical
Grew dimmer in our sight.

Long before the dawn we'd peeled
The layers from the onion
Of I and you and he and she
And it, and we, and One.

I dreamed of vales and mountains,
Pale moons and downy thickets
Where roseate nymphs were hotly pursued
By horned definitions.

The sun of noon beat on my eyes
When I woke between bed and wall;
She'd gathered her selves and left me there
Not feeling myself at all.

# Michael Hartnett
# (Micheál Ó hAirtnéide)

b. 1941

## SSU K'UNG T'U WALKS IN THE FOREST

*A version of his twenty-four poems*
*for Liam Brady*

1   The soul that rests has riches:
    death in motion, bourgeois man.
    I walked along the wood-track
    with an old knapsack of truths,
    by deserts and by spring wells
    with an old knapsack of truths.

2   Quietnesss of the high flight
    of the solitary crane,
    of rustles of a silk robe,
    of coveted sweetnesses,
    of elusive bamboo flutes:
    a thing we cannot pocket.

3   Gathering green watercress,
    I saw a beautiful girl,
    willows, peach-trees, orioles,
    reality, and such things:
    I embraced those infinite
    and those ancient miracles.

4   The green pines in the clear air,
    I take off my cap and walk
    under branches of birds' song.
    No wild geese in the clear air,
    but through the moonlit barriers
    I could converse with my love.

5   And the god with lotus hands
    passed, to the neighbouring moon:
    Mount Hua shouldering the dark
    and bronze silence from its bell.
    I saw a lunar halo
    around his calm lotus hands.

6   In rain a gentle cleric
    writing his flower-poems.
    Hints of birds in the bamboo,
    his lute in a green twilight.
    In rain a gentle cleric
    still as a chrysanthemum.

7   "Take the iron from your heart:
    contemplate familiar stars,
    do not underrate the moon-
    beam as a form of transport:
    go back as light as child's steps
    to your lunar yesterdays.

8   "Be vital as the rainbow
    among the tall hills of Wu:
    let the winds billow your silk:
    keep Force as food in the soul:
    create but do not grow less:
    as the rainbow, give and live.

9   "If the mind has pearl inset,
    what is gold to river mist,
    to a branch of almond flowers,
    to a painted bridge in mist,
    to a friend at lute-music?
    Simple things empearl the mind.

10  "Be wary of scrutiny,
    of climbing mountains to look
    down on birds, on waterfalls.
    Do not climb up trees to see

a minute flower open.
Bow: it will be on the ground.

11  "All creation by your side,
the simple sun, moon and stars:
even a vagrant phoenix
and a tame leviathan.
God is not as far as Good:
open your palm, rain falls in.

12  "The poet can live outside
of print, but if his own song
cannot make him cry, if he
is not his first and finest
audience, then he merely
writes small words down on petals.

13  "That they might always come back
and be with us forever!
Bright river and bright parrot,
the stranger from the dark hill:
without the ash of writing,
may they always be with us!

14  "All words should be as things are:
artistic as flowers budding,
limpid as dew, important
as wide roads to horizons:
words should be as green as spring
as like moonlight as is snow.

15  "I sit here under the pines
reading the old poetry,
heeding only day and dark,
unaware of the seasons,
happy, poor and literate:
an old man waiting for God."

16  Confronted by such repose,
my mind quits its tenement

and walks after its love: she
glides like a jade figurine,
her greenness into the glade,
becoming the glade, its light.

17  I climbed the T'ai-Hsing mountain
and I made a small echo.
The trees were like seas of jade,
flower-scent almost opaque:
I heard it rebound from the
waterfall, the same echo.

18  With plain words for simple thoughts
did I not touch the heart of
Tao? For I saw a poet,
a man with sticks on his back,
a man listening to music,
and I had not searched for them.

19  She whom I asked will not come
and I am bitter as death.
Centuries die in the glade
and Tao is passing away:
whom shall we ask salvation?
Wind whistles, leaf falls, rain falls.

20  I held his image inside,
like the image of all waves,
of all green things, all blossoms,
all the barrenness of hills.
To have likeness without form,
is that to possess the man?

21  I plunged arm up to elbow
in a pile of damp green moss,
in broken tendrils almost
found it: and found it almost
listening to the oriole.
Elusive as a rainbow!

22   Never about to be grasped:
     like the white crane of Mount Hou
     like the white cloud of Mount Hua
     like vigour in old portraits
     of the armed ancient heroes:
     just about to be disclosed.

23   Life can be a hundred years:
     drinking wine from fine goblets,
     talking with our oldest friends,
     visiting flower-gardens
     strolling with a staff of thorn
     —but look at that great mountain!

24   I have made a simple song
     walking now in the forest,
     song of the Mighty Centre
     —like pearls rolling on a floor?
     —like turns of a water-wheel?
     Explanations are for fools.

*Dublin, 1970*


## I SAW MAGIC ON A GREEN COUNTRY ROAD ...

I saw magic on a green country road—
That old woman, a bag of sticks her load,

Blackly down to her thin feet a fringed shawl,
A rosary of bone on her horned hand,
A flight of curlews scribing by her head,
And ashtrees combing with their frills her hair.

Her eyes, wet sunken holes pierced by an awl,
Must have deciphered her adoring land:
And curlews, no longer lean birds, instead
Become ten scarlet comets in the air.

Some incantation from her canyoned mouth,
Irish, English, blew frost along the ground,
And even though the wind was from the South
The ashleaves froze without an ashleaf sound.


## I HAVE EXHAUSTED
## THE DELIGHTED RANGE ...


I have exhausted the delighted range
of small birds, and now, a new end to pain
makes a mirage of what I wished my life.
torture, immediate to me, is strange:
all that is left of the organs remain
in an anaesthetic of unbelief.

coerced by trivia, nothing to gain
but now, or to be pleased through one long night

and forsake instead something immortal?
and the graceless heron is killed in flight
and falls like a lopped flower into the stalks.

small birds, small poems are not immortal;
nor, however passed, is one intense night.
there is no time now for my dream of hawks.


## THE OAT WOMAN


She heard the gates of autumn
        splinter into ash
grey shock of toppling insects
        as the gate broke down.
Old nails in their nests of rust
        screamed at this swivel:

booted limbs of working men
    walked on her body.
Their coats lay down in sculpture,
    each with a tired dog:
thin blades quaked at blunt whetstones:
    purple barked at blue.
The whetstones drank their water
    and flayed the bright edge.
Each oat like sequin shivered:
    her gold body tensed,
fear lapped across her acre
    in a honey wave
and buckets of still porter
    turned to discs of black.
Iron and stone called warning
    to her shaking ears:
arms enforced a fierce caress,
    brown and blind and bronze.
Sickles drove her back and back
    to a golden wedge;
her hissing beads fell silent
    in dead yellow bands.
Across her waist the reaping
    whipped like silver moons,
wind whistled banked flute laments,
    musical sweat fell.
Animals left in terror
    pheasant, sparrow, hare
deserting her in anguish,
    crowding from her skirts.
She curled in a golden fear
    on the last headland,
the sad outline of her breasts
    bare through the oatstalks.
Four arms took sickles and swung—
    no single killer:
she vanished from the shorn field
    in that red autumn.

# PIGKILLING

Like a knife cutting a knife
his last plea for life
echoes joyfully in Camas.
An egg floats
like a navel
in the pickling-barrel:
before he sinks,
his smiling head
sees a delicate girl
up to her elbows
in a tub of blood
while the avalanche
of his offal steams
among the snapping dogs
and mud
and porksteaks
coil in basins
like bright snakes
and buckets of boiling water hiss
to soften his bristles
for the blade.
I kick his golden bladder
in the air.
It lands like a moon
among the damsons.
Like a knife cutting a knife
his last plea for life
echoes joyfully in Camas.

*Camas*: a townland five miles south of Newcastle West
in Co. Limerick where I spent most of my childhood.

## DEATH OF AN IRISHWOMAN

Ignorant, in the sense
she ate monotonous food
and thought the world was flat,
and pagan, in the sense
she knew the things that moved
at night were neither dogs nor cats
but púcas and darkfaced men
she nevertheless had fierce pride.
But sentenced in the end
to eat thin diminishing porridge
in a stone-cold kitchen
she clenched her brittle hands
around a world
she could not understand.
I loved her from the day she died.
She was a summer dance at the crossroads.
She was a cardgame where a nose was broken.
She was a song that nobody sings.
She was a house ransacked by soldiers.
She was a language seldom spoken.
She was a child's purse, full of useless things.


## *from* A FAREWELL TO ENGLISH

### *for Brendan Kennelly*

I

Her eyes were coins of porter and her West
Limerick voice talked velvet in the house:
her hair was black as the glossy fireplace
wearing with grace her Sunday-night-dance best.
She cut the froth from glasses with a knife
and hammered golden whiskies on the bar
and her mountainy body tripped the gentle
mechanism of verse: the minute interlock
of word and word began, the rhythm formed.

I sunk my hands into tradition
sifting the centuries for words. This quiet
excitement was not new: emotion challenged me
to make it sayable. The clichés came
at first, like matchsticks snapping from the world
of work: mánla, séimh, dubhfholtach, álainn, caoin:
they came like grey slabs of slate breaking from
an ancient quarry, mánla, séimh, dubhfholtach,
álainn, caoin, slowly vaulting down the dark
unused escarpments, mánla, séimh, dubhfholtach,
álainn, caoin, crashing on the cogs, splinters
like axeheads damaging the wheels, clogging
the intricate machine, mánla, séimh,
dubhfholtach, álainn, caoin. Then Pegasus
pulled up, the girth broke and I was flung back
on the gravel of Anglo-Saxon.
What was I doing with these foreign words?
I, the polisher of the complex clause,
wizard of grasses and warlock of birds
midnight-oiled in the metric laws?


3

Chef Yeats, that master of the use of herbs
could raise mere stew to a glorious height,
pinch of saga, soupçon of philosophy
carefully stirred in to get the flavour right,
and cook a poem around the basic verbs.
Our commis-chefs attend and learn the trade,
bemoan the scraps of Gaelic that they know:
add to a simple Anglo-Saxon stock
Cuchulainn's marrow-bones to marinate,
a dash of Ó Rathaille simmered slow,
a glass of University hic-haec-hoc:
sniff and stand back and proudly offer you
the celebrated Anglo-Irish stew.

*dubhfholtach*: blacklocked. *álainn*: beautiful. *mánla, séimh* and *caoin*:
words whose meanings hover about the English adjectives graceful,
gentle.

6

Gaelic is the conscience of our leaders,
the memory of a mother-rape they will
not face, the heap of bloody rags they see
and scream at in their boardrooms of mock oak.
They push us towards the world of total work,
our politicians with their seedy minds
and dubious labels, Communist or
Capitalist, none wanting freedom—
only power. All that reminds us
we are human and therefore not a herd
must be concealed or killed or slowly left
to die, or microfilmed to waste no space.
For Gaelic is our final sign that
we are human, therefore not a herd.

I saw our governments the other night—
I think the scene was Leopardstown—
horribly deformed dwarfs rode the racetrack
each mounted on a horribly deformed dwarf:
greenfaced, screaming, yellow-toothed, prodding
each other with electric prods, thrashing
each others' skinny arses, dribbling snot
and smeared with their own dung, they galloped
towards the prize, a glass and concrete anus.

I think the result was a dead heat.


*from* CÚLÚ ÍDE

Dhein fearthainn na hoíche glib
mharmair dhuibh ar a ceann
is bhí ribe liath amháin
ina scamh gheal airgid ann.

Gág dhomhain amháin ina clár
éadain, snoite ann le fuath
ag scoilteadh cearnóg a cinn,
sreang péine greamaithe go dlúth.

A malaí tanaí mar lorg pinn
buailte go beacht, cruinn ar phár
ribe i ndiadh ribe go slím
—obair shaoir ghlic gan cháim.

Bhí a srón róchnámhach, nocht
is a haghaidh bhocht mar aghaidh scáil:
le gáire aerach ní théadh
rós a polláirí riamh i mbláth.

Bhí réaltaí beaga óir
i ngormlóchrann a súl,
súile a pósadh ar mhaithe le spré
is nach bhfuair ach mórfhuath.

Bhí líne álainn ar a beol
uachtar mar órchlúmh bog éin:
i mborradh ramhar an bheoil
íochtair shoilsigh deoir an léin.

Smig agus giall mín nár lag;
cnámha teannmhúnláilte faoi shnua,
cnámha beaga, lúbacha, briosca
mar chloigeann fiosach mhadra rua.

Bhí a scornach bhán gan sian
gan roic na haoise, gan líon
féitheog; gan fealltóir mná
le feiceáil sa cholún mín
Bhí gach ball eile clúdaithe faoi dhubh-olla a gúna.

## *from* THE RETREAT OF ITA CAGNEY

Moulded to a wedge of jet
by the wet night, her black hair
showed one grey rib, like a fine
steel filing on a forge floor.
One deep line, cut by silent
days of hate in the expanse
of sallow skin above her brows,
dipped down to a tragic slant.
Her eyebrows were thin penlines
finely drawn on parchment sheets,
hair after minuscule hair
a linear masterpiece.
Triangles of minute gold
broke her open blue of eyes
that had looked on bespoke love,
seeing only to despise.
Her long nose was almost bone
making her face too severe:
the tight and rose-edged nostrils
never belled into a flare.
A fine gold down above the
upper lip did not maintain
its prettiness nor lower's swell
make it less a graph of pain.
Chin and jawline delicate,
neither weak nor skeletal:
bone in definite stern mould,
small and strong like a fox-skull.
Her throat showed no signs of age.
No sinews reinforced flesh
or gathered in clenched fistfuls
to pull skin to lined mesh.

The rest was shapeless, in black woollen dress.

*translated by the author*

# Eiléan Ní Chuilleanáin

b. 1942


## LUCINA SCHYNNING IN SILENCE
## OF THE NICHT ...

Moon shining in silence of the night
The heaven being all full of stars
I was reading my book in a ruin
By a sour candle, without roast meat or music
Strong drink or a shield from the air
Blowing in the crazed window, and I felt
Moonlight on my head, clear after three days' rain.

I washed in cold water; it was orange, channelled down bogs
Dipped between cresses.
The bats flew through my room where I slept safely.
Sheep stared at me when I woke.

Behind me the waves of darkness lay, the plague
Of mice, plague of beetles
Crawling out of the spines of books,
Plague shadowing pale faces with clay
The disease of the moon gone astray.

In the desert I relaxed, amazed
As the mosaic beasts on the chapel floor
When Cromwell had departed, and they saw
The sky growing through the hole in the roof.

Sheepdogs embraced me; the grasshopper
Returned with lark and bee.
I looked down between hedges of high thorn and saw
The hare, absorbed, sitting still
In the middle of the track; I heard
Again the chirp of the stream running.

# WASH

Wash man out of the earth; shear off
The human shell.
Twenty feet down there's close cold earth
So clean.

Wash the man out of the woman;
The strange sweat from her skin, the ashes from her hair.
Stretch her to dry in the sun
The blue marks on her breast will fade.

Woman and world not yet
Clean as the cat
Leaping to the windowsill with a fish in her teeth;
Her flat curious eyes reflect the squalid room,
She begins to wash the water from the fish.


# SWINEHERD

"When all this is over," said the swineherd,
"I mean to retire, where
Nobody will have heard about my special skills
And conversation is mainly about the weather.

I intend to learn how to make coffee, at least as well
As the Portuguese lay-sister in the kitchen
And polish the brass fenders every day.
I want to lie awake at night
Listening to cream crawling to the top of the jug
And the water lying soft in the cistern.

I want to see an orchard where the trees grow in straight lines
And the yellow fox finds shelter between the navy-blue trunks,
Where it gets dark early in summer
And the apple-blossom is allowed to wither on the bough."

## THE SECOND VOYAGE

Odysseus rested on his oar and saw
The ruffled foreheads of the waves
Crocodiling and mincing past: he rammed
The oar between their jaws and looked down
In the simmering sea where scribbles of weed defined
Uncertain depth, and the slim fishes progressed
In fatal formation, and thought
                        If there was a single
Streak of decency in these waves now, they'd be ridged
Pocked and dented with the battering they've had,
And we could name them as Adam named the beasts,
Saluting a new one with dismay, or a notorious one
With admiration; they'd notice us passing
And rejoice at our shipwreck, but these
Have less character than sheep and need more patience.

I know what I'll do he said;
I'll park my ship in the crook of a long pier
(And I'll take you with me he said to the oar)
I'll face the rising ground and walk away
From tidal waters, up riverbeds
Where herons parcel out the miles of stream,
Over gaps in the hills, through warm
Silent valleys, and when I meet a farmer
Bold enough to look me in the eye
With "where are you off to with that long
Winnowing fan over your shoulder?"
There I will stand still
And I'll plant you for a gatepost or a hitching-post
And leave you as a tidemark. I can go back
And organise my house then.
                      But the profound
Unfenced valleys of the ocean still held him;
He had only the oar to make them keep their distance;
The sea was still frying under the ship's side.
He considered the water-lilies, and thought about fountains

Spraying as wide as willows in empty squares,
The sugarstick of water clattering into the kettle,
The flat lakes bisecting the rushes. He remembered spiders
   and frogs
Housekeeping at the roadside in brown trickles floored with
   mud,
Horsetroughs, the black canal, pale swans at dark:
His face grew damp with tears that tasted
Like his own sweat or the insults of the sea.


## GOING BACK TO OXFORD


Something to lose; it came in the equipment
Alongside the suicide pill and the dark blue card:
"I am a Catholic, please send for a priest"
With a space below for the next of kin.

Something to lose; and going back to Oxford,
Though not for good this time, I lose it again
As the city advances like an old relation
It's no use insulting.
Notice how she repeats her effects,
The Victorian towers after the mediaeval slum,
As a yawn turns into a shiver and the air
Bites like a mould pulling me north
To the evacuated roads.
Here the eye shrinks from what it sees,
The toothmarks are showing where the sharp spires got me;
And I agree to being chewed because
All that time I was looking for a reliable experience
And here it is: I give in every time,
Repeat the original despair.
This is where I learned it.

Because pleasure is astonishing, but loss
Expected, never at a loss for words;
Tearducts built in at birth: something to lose:

The best kind of innocence, which is not to have been afraid,
Lost according to plan; and here I am, walking
Through old streets to a familiar bed.


## THE LADY'S TOWER

Hollow my high tower leans
Back to the cliff; my thatch
Converses with spread sky,
Heronries. The grey wall
Slices downward and meets
A sliding flooded stream
Pebble-banked, small diving
Birds. Downstairs my cellars plumb.

Behind me shifting the oblique veins
Of the hill; my kitchen is damp,
Spiders shaded under brown vats.

I hear the stream change pace, glance from the stove
To see the punt is now floating freely
Bobs square-ended, the rope dead-level.

Opening the kitchen door
The quarry brambles miss my hair
Sprung so high their fruit wastes.

And up the tall stairs my bed is made
Even with a sycamore root
At my small square window.

All night I lie sheeted, my broom chases down treads
Delighted spirals of dust: the yellow duster glides
Over shelves, around knobs: bristle stroking flagstone
Dancing with the spiders around the kitchen in the dark
While cats climb the tower and the river fills
A spoonful of light on the cellar walls below.

## OLD ROADS

Missing from the map, the abandoned roads
Reach across the mountain, threading into
Clefts and valleys, shuffle between thick
Hedges of flowery thorn.
The grass flows into tracks of wheels,
Mowed evenly by the careful sheep;
Drenched, it guards the gaps of silence
Only trampled on the pattern day.

And if, an odd time, late
At night, a cart passes
Splashing in a burst stream, crunching bones,
The wavering candle hung by the shaft
Slaps light against a single gable
Catches a flat tombstone
Shaking a nervous beam in a white face

Their arthritic fingers
Their stiffening grasp cannot
Hold long on the hillside—
Slowly the old roads lose their grip.

## ODYSSEUS MEETS THE GHOSTS
## OF THE WOMEN

There also he saw
The celebrated women
And in death they looked askance;
He stood and faced them,
Shadows flocked by the dying ram
To sup the dark blood flowing at his heel
—His long sword fending them off,
Their whispering cold
Their transparent grey throats from the lifeblood.

He saw the daughters, wives
Mothers of heroes or upstanding kings
The longhaired goldbound women who had died
Of pestilence, famine, in slavery
And still queens but they did not know
His face, even Anticleia
His own mother. He asked her how she died
But she passed by his elbow, her eyes asleep.

The hunter still followed
Airy victims, and labour
Afflicted even here the cramped shoulders—
The habit of distress.

A hiss like thunder, all their voices
Broke on him; he fled
For the long ship, the evening sea
Persephone's poplars
And her dark willow trees.


## A GENTLEMAN'S BEDROOM

Those long retreating shades,
A river of roofs inclining
In the valley side. Gables and stacks
And spires, with trees tucked between them:
All graveyard shapes
Viewed from his high windowpane.

A coffin-shaped looking-glass replies,
Soft light, polished, smooth as fur,
Blue of mown grass on a lawn,
With neckties crookedly doubled over it.

Opening the door, all walls point at once to the bed
Huge red silk in a quarter of the room

Knots drowning in deep mahogany
And uniform blue volumes shelved at hand.

And a desk calendar, a fountain-pen,
A weighty table-lighter in green marble,
A cigar-box, empty but dusted,
A framed young woman in a white dress
Indicate the future from the cold mantel.

The house sits silent,
The shiny linoleum
Would creak if you stepped on it.
Outside it is still raining
But the birds have begun to sing.

# Augustus Young

b. 1943

## HERITAGE

*(the verb 'to have' does not exist in Gaelic)*

One cannot possess
the house until the death
of a father, until the old man,
cutting a twist by the fire,
fails to fill the bowl,
lays down the pipe
or sometimes luckily enough
shovels himself into the earth.

One must not appear to own the place
until the first grass covers the grave.

Then you have it
and the land—one acre in ten
of arable bog. But you cannot possess
a wife until your mother
accepts the death and, in many a case,
accepts her own. There is no choice.

This is being a true son.
Allow the country die for you.

## LAST REFUGE

We brushed our hair back and our
sideburns down. Drainpipes
tight as the gripe. Tongues too tough
for words (longer than four letters). Flick-knives
and bicycle chains, we had. And mothers
pleading at the Juveniles: trouble because
we slashed the backseats of the 'gods'.

Our hands, ringed like prize-cocks,
trembled when caught by the sleeve.
We said, "Have a fag," and, "Leave
us alone." Chained to our slogans, we scratched
blackheads, like pilgrims out of Bunyan.

When Elvis went soft, we gave away to women.
Joined up 'Overseas'. Wars and discharge won,
registered love. This is our dominion—
slippers and hatchets before the television.


## from MR THACKERAY ON CORK

> A verse translation of William Makepeace Thackeray's
> *Irish Sketch Book* (1843)

### POPULAR CONDITIONS

Though picturesque, Coalmarket Street
is quite another world indeed:
tatterdemalion stalls with clothes
(the castoff wardrobes of scarecrows):
where shawlie women in spirehats
brew poteens from the innards of rats
while giving suck to scabrous babies
and beating off dogs with rabies.

Here wideboys bide the time of day
in long tailed coats of hoddin-grey,
corduroy breeches, and shod in shoes
that raise a mighty dust; in their twos
flourishing donnybrook sticks. Crime
keeps the police out. The dying
are dragged to Half Moon Street and pegged
to the railings and there anointed.

Two minutes away, the Grand Parade
enjoys a different kind of trade:
in smart arcades, no bustle,
perfumed goods brought to skirt rustle,
lackeys and landaus, all the show
of wealth, in fact. While a stone's throw
would open up a human sewer,
the pandemonium of the poor.

Still charity has not a hope.
A beggar lad to whom I spoke
told me, he'd rather rape and steal
from his mother than be wheeled
into a job—shipped in shackles
to the Welsh mines, breaking one's back till
home means the workhouse—I've my pride.
Hell is to die on the other side.

It's wise to stay on. Not a bad
place to be jailed in, or go mad.
The Asylum's clean, has a good name
for its happy clinking of chains.
Healthier in than out. Lose your mind
and they'll mind your body. You'll find
inmates daily get milk and bread
and a safe place to lay their head.

The County Jail is better still,
a haven for the criminal,
with solid walls and solider meals:
the authorities don't want Bastilles.
And where malefactors are concerned,
they give them what cannot be earned
honestly—hunger is the norm
in this town: too many are born.

### THEOBALD MATHEW (TEMPERANCE LEADER)

The ladies love him: this good priest,
stoutly handsome, with not the least
trace of draconian demeanour
expected of a Temperance weaner.
No 'small beer'. Almost a Whig. Views
moderate. A listener, who'd choose
common-sense. Not given to preach.
We had tea with him (one cup each).

### THE URSULINE CONVENT (A PERSONAL VIEW)

The Best Families (on the decline)
put daughters in the Ursuline
Convent. So how could I refuse
an invite there, despite my views.
On the drive, blossoming-potatoes,
'La Violette' on two pianos
greet me—it's the young ladies who
are schooled there for a London debut.

The hallbell responds to my touch:
chords crash; and, in hardly as much
as a quaver-rest, playing resumes,
though more subdued, in distant rooms—
Grand Pianos everywhere. More
life here than a broth. . . . The door
opens. A nun ushers me in,
not meeting my eye, for fear of sin,

a conspiracy between us
(O Naples Bay when Vesuvius
erupts). Hush-hush to the parlour.
There a vegetable odour
seeps. And unearthly bad taste too:
expensive canvases, brand new,
framed in brocade . . . I don't feel well.
The abbess shows me to the chapel

where postulants peek behind grilles,
disturbed in prayer. Nuns make me feel
uneasy. Draped in shapeless sheets,
how do they move—it can't be feet.
Not as other women whose life
gives life: death has them as a wife. . . .
I had to leave: to breathe the air
of Monkstown across the river.

# Pádraig J. Daly

b. 1943

## SUMMERS IN DONERAILE

At night there was no stairs
Between us and activity;
We fell asleep listening to the talk in the kitchen
And woke to the ticking of the clock
And the faint perfume of Christmas soap.
The canon's photograph hung above the mantelpiece
Drawing the whole house into its serenity.

My grandmother sat on a high armchair
And told us how he died and how they
Spread straw on the roadway
To save him from the creak of wheels.

He had written about the people she knew:
Neighbours, friends of friends, even a cousin
Of her own. She remembered being in town once
When first copies arrived; and a washerwoman
He had celebrated brought the news from shop to shop.
People came smiling to their doorways
Like a Barry wedding or a Confirmation Day.

On Sundays we walked to mass.
There was a footpath with wide grassbanks
Along the mile from Brough. Spancelled goats
And cows grazed there. The canon, Grandma said,
Strolled that mile at evening. Did Murphy's
Offwhite gander or its ancestor
Terrorise him?

Each year we made the pilgrimage from Leary's
Gate to Glenanaar. We ate sandwiches
Near Nodlaig's Bridge. Further down, a river
Raced over the road on cobblestones; we took heather
From its banks and stones for the rock garden.

Other poets found silence in this countryside.
Once Spenser owned everywhere we walked
And the gentle Bregogue which ran below our fields
Had like a courtly lady deceived him.
Behind the tall windows of Bowenscourt
A woman in black ferreted through the deepest
Crevices of the heart and lit a candle
For travellers on the Winter roadways.

But it was the canon who reared our imaginations
Most of all and taught us love for the quiet about us,
The green calm (unbroken by any sea)
Of Muskerry fields and the dogs barking at foxes at evening.


COOLROE


There were views of Killarney on the postcards
We sold in the shop with grassy islands
In lakes and symmetrical clouds painted
Onto a blue sky.
They reminded me of Coolroe Cross: two grassy mounds
Moving silently onto grey tar, clouds overhead.

After the bus the road was straight for a mile.
We turned off at the top of the hill. In the fine weather
It took all day to travel: we loitered
Over blackberries, sucked fuschia for honey or rooted
Between the fraoch for hurts. In winter we stepped on ice
Till it cracked and rivulets spread out on the dust road.

As you came close, the house disappeared
But for one red window through an arch of fuchsia
And thorn. The gate (dragging when you pushed)
Was wide enough for horse and dray.
There was always a dog to create a commotion
Of fowl; the bees made a racket overhead.

It was Redmond country: there were no patriots on view;
The queen of England rode horse on a biscuit box.
Sitting by the fireplace, we smelled in the broken turf
All the dying of old forests. There was much dying:
Irish was spoken only when there was something we were not to
    know;
We listened slyly and brought the news home.

The winters are clearest: my father wrapping us in big coats,
Making us forms in the grassy bank like leverets;
My aunt talking to a neighbour, complaining of the cold;
While we watched lonely lamps along the hillsides,
Counted stars, waiting for our palace of floating light,
The journey downhill, the suddenness of the sea.

# John Ennis

b. 1944

## SGARÚINT NA gCOMPÁNACH*

Abruptly, soon after breakfast, you departed, food
Gulped, at dawn this morning. Cratered moon petered
Out at its zenith. Cold fists of blue deterred
Clouds from the sky. I had meant to say good
Bye offering a gift by which no heaven, hell
Would separate us ever. When I knocked, no reply
Helloed. Running downstairs I saw the car already
Take you. A few hands were raised in farewell.

I walked upstairs, went in your room. In it cruel disarray:
Smells of the bitter afterbirth, your sudden removal
Out of our lives. On your bed I sat, saw it all:
Christmas in Clough '62, skating on its frozen lakes in bleak
    array;
June '63 torrential showers, the daft seas, waves we wore
Clothes tucked under stonewalls; precious rock-haunt lures;
Spirit of Connemara, Torc, the greenwood tours.
I closed the door on what could be no more.

This chilled day of autumn oaks I found no peace at all.
First frosts have inflamed the close September leaves.
Constant in its garish space my mind bleeps, grieves.
Your absence haunts. That speeding car. I recall
Your face at my door, asking a request,
Hard confidences uttered at the end,
That extraordinary flair for etching: when your Christ
Became you at the lintel. I did not comprehend.

*'The Parting of Companions' [ed.]

I rose, dressed at small hours. "Am I my brother's guardian?"
And I had dreamt one in sweat. Black soured caws of crows
Streamed round their creaking beech. Leaves beat my
    window's
Vitreous face. I saw your model aeroplane crash. Cain
Threw wide my salt-raw room in cold harangues.
Without, two joy-drunk hares sported (as our last night
Died). Lawn was all theirs. Clouds veiled the moon. Delight
Exulted: one tumbled, ravished the other. No jaws bared fangs.

Henry, accept this pale proffered In Memoriam.
I heard you once cry anger at all ritual
(As we polished gold chalices of the lamb)
That gilds the speechless throat, each cleavered call.
These lines cut us somewhat in cross-section,
Engrave the blank metal plates with what was sure.
I tidy your drawing board too, our affection.
Translate your love into life's architecture.


## BIRTH AT AIRMOUNT

*for Anne*

You've left me now. Hot foot
I'm told to stay put.
From your second-floor maternity
Window I see, and do not see,
Silence brooding across old Corporation
Houses, smoky chimney pots, 2nd of June
Congress Place;
Cattleless, the hosed mart at high Ballybricken
Straggle of summer lovers past the Dole House to the Regina,
Two French ships anchoring on the placid Suir at seven-thirty
Mooring ropes of the cargo vessels dropping over bollards,
Woodcock's coo gently buoyant in thinly greying
Bluish clouds . . .
                    Down in The Glen Imelda Bolger's
                    Calling her two eldest in.

Squabbles,
Terrace roofs ads for orange fibre glass hardly insulate,
The ageing jute men unemployed with sons in AnCo,
Marriages on the verge, daughters out for a Glass
Craftsman, most settling for young apprentices.
Hearts trust all in Tomorrow here and the IDA.*

Woodcock and its twilight over gardens are hanging
In delicate imbalance. A magnolia blooms across from Coady's
Love, assortment of voices
—If love means to feed, clothe, see red, soothe
A toothache when the black liquorice hits the nerve—

Love
Rummaging the minor memorabilia of a Summer's day
Squads of after-supper threes to tens to seventeens
On chalked pavements. No ground for sport.
Bed. Kitchen. Mother tried to gas a family
One cold Sunday morning. Facing a bleak table.

                  *

Sun was loitering in the East that terrible Sunday
Attempted its first frail kicks in your womb.

The minutes are taking their
Deadly time. One o'clock on I've watched
Anatomy of pain, drip, pethidine, blood oozing.

My palms polished with the constant friction
Shine like the corridors' parquet flooring.
Tidy small of your back's an old washing board.
Venus, a shorn mound of swollen rending flesh.
Cries like raw bile topped up your silky throat.

Minute by minute savagery. Verse is a cold
Travesty. Drip forced you.
Drooped in a wheelchair you were whisked
To delivery couch.

*IDA: Industrial Development Authority [ed.]

"I'm ready."

*

On a hospital cherry, a blackbird blossoms into late tune.
Congress Place intrudes, swells, ebbs round your June
Bed. 7.40 p.m.

If to your expulsive travail my ear's a foetal stethoscope
I praise those (Goretti with Ergometrine) who must hourly
   cope:
Fionnuala, Barbara, Eileen, Joan, Kathleen, thanks;
Gallagher, the doctor, easing the baby out safely, thanks.

Miss Egg Head, in an inkling, sits on your diaphragm
(To whom I'm a blur or nothing at all). She's swaddled, warm
To touch. If I say she has my dead father's face,
Who knows. Yours, truly, of all that agony, bears not a trace.


## A DRINK OF SPRING

After the sweat of swathes and the sinking madder sun
The clean-raked fields of a polychrome twilight
With cloudlets of indigo nomadic on the sky,
"A drink of spring" was my father's preface to the night.

As the youngest, I made fast the dairy-window reins,
Sent the galvanised bucket plummeting to sink first
Time, weighted with steel washers at one frost-patterned side.
His request was as habitual as a creaking kitchen joist.

The rope tautened for the upward pull under the damson
Tree and the back-biting thorns of a never-pruned rose.
The water, laced with lime, was glacial to the dusty throat.
Mirage of the dying, it brings relief to the lips of the comatose.

Cups furred with cold I handed round the open-door fireless
Kitchen. The taste on my lips was lingering like a first kiss.

# HOLY HOUR

Rose Coyne of Chapel Cross donated the Sanctuary Calvary.
The dead and gone faithful of the nineteenth-century poor
Hoarded their golds and cool Crucifixion blues for the chapel.
We knelt out the Holy Hour mid-way between altar and door.

Bird song saturates those sun-sinking evenings of childhood.
Familiar rouged cheeks of Annunciation and Resurrection
    faces
Glowed while the blackbirds and thrushes quarrelled in yews
Bickering in our ears over their graveyard nesting places.

The nerves of our curate had been shattered in the War.
My report marks once elicited his mild surprise.
He'd handed me a Latin primer for the Secondary.
A cascade of white doves fell fluttering from his eyes.

In London he'd seen a War-scarred minister pause
To feed news-hungry reporters, issue them a brief,
The darkening import of his troubled countenance,
"Why, I do believe, I've lost my handkerchief!"

Matt Cahill talked of the black ritual he had seen,
A lady, nationalistic, battle-time fervent in the extreme
Befouling the haggard face of a German prisoner. Of all
Evil, this, for him, cried out the most foul spittle-venomous
    crime.

He'd travelled Europe, watched it die. I heard the judgement-
Day Nazis move cell to cell torturing the world's unclean.
Serpent bit Christendom to the core. His slimy head
The nymph-like blue virgin crushed now, smiled saccharine.

Matt Cahill died young. Little trace of the honours graduate
Gilt his syllables. His frail white frame shuddered.
    Remembrance
Doubted which was the more savage reality in the early sixties,
Blitz, or the eyes in our herded faces glazed with incognisance.

He cast us lights from the altar rails. Mother-of-Pearl people
Yawned as a final blast of roseate sun lit up the saints and their
   sets
Of glory. Two surpliced boys ran for the monstrance box.
There was a rustle of kissed beads slipped into pockets.

A handful of girls and Owen Judge, the sweetest tenor in
   Coralstown
Rose to *O Salutaris*, the honeyed strains of *Tantum Ergo*.
The incense of gold vowels was blown across our heads.
We bowed to the flowery altar and the throbbing censer.

Today the singers clustered in the organ loft are quiet on
   Sundays,
Look down no more on where we murmured the prayers, our
   place
Guaranteed mid-way between altar and door, upset by no
   crackle
Or gossip of guns. As we knelt, we spat into nobody's face.

Outside, in hundreds, the yard-dead loosened their bones
That yellowed fragmentary in once wooden boxes. Unsung
At the back wall by the laurels lay my father's people.
As we left, memories of the heart would germinate on his
   tongue.

# BAD FRIDAY

1

The brightness of the ward hit you like a pig-axe
On the forehead as you woke when we arrived by the bed.
Killer of pigs, you once stood master of this terror.

A stoat slid sleekly out from under the bed sheet,
Sucked your thin stubbled neck in front of our eyes,
Haunts the lingering scene words still shy from in tears.

The clutch of the pale heaving drowned was yours.
We walked deeper into the marketplace of the sea
Mirroring the helpless beast of consciousness.

2

Your mouth tried to yoke syllables like an old plough team,
Root us buried phrases from a January tillage.
Your broad-acred chest shuddered for words.

Your tongue could not sheaf speech like a reaper.
We brought low like a shower the blaze of your grain.
The harvest of your affection was lodged and lost.

I clasped the hand that was once a mainstay.
Its puffed joints twitched for us beneath the clothes,
Whether in welcome or good-bye I do not know.

3

The bed sores were raw on your buttocks and heels.
The ordeals outside death's locked door unmanned you.
Lengths of functional thin tubing shamed your pot stomach.

Your eyes fixed hard on us. Tear them out. Let me die.
Instead we propped you up, deafened you with whispers.
Bacteria of light and dark rattled in the windpipe.

We wiped your rusty spittle clean, mopped the brow
Saw your intelligence bill-hook a brain-torn path
Back to us through an opiate growth of briars.


4

You clambered from the renal bog. Manhood was still
A force in the diaphragm, loins and warm boles of the thigh.
The latter hardened every day a more inexorable lead.

"Don't upset yourself." Your face winced on our emetic cheer.
Blessing drawn from a visiting cleric drugged you.
The soutane whisked off as your slack mouth opened on
    repose.

Forgive clay thoughts in a clay head. Afraid you'd wake
Suffer another stroke, we settled for a karstland in the mind.
We were not sons but vandals melting from your side.


ALL OVER

Sunlight was niggling in the cloudy sky as we motored in
To see you. Using a forceps and swabs of cotton wool
We soothed your broken lips and swollen tongue with
    glycerine.

A weakling cough brought up spittle. Your blue eyes were dull,
Did not know us or see the busy white-capped nurses weave
Between the beds with syringes and devotion. The ward was
    full.

I remember how your gums did tighten on each swab and
    cleave
To it for sustenance. The simple glycerine proved a boon
For your mouth's hydrated sores. We were obliged to leave

As two nurses came to bed-bath you. Later, on the afternoon
Journey out to the hospital, keeping your plight to the fore,
We bought you a small purple towel and baby dribbler in
   Dunne's

Stores. Such was the bitter menial language of the love we bore
You. You spared us that. Nurses had just turned your body
Over from left to right. A NO VISITORS sign hung crookedly
   on the blue door.

An orderly opened the medical ward for us at two-thirty.
The April sun illuminated the sick beds with its brevities,
Sparkled on sterile gallipots and cylinders on a trolley.

No doubt it was your slumped pallor took us by surprise
As we approached you. Patients, propped up in beds around,
Stared into Buddha-country. Some smoked, a well-fed
   resignation in their eyes.

Your mouth fell slack, opening to us without a sound,
The tip of the tongue drooled through your lips and hung
Loosely there when we touched your blank-page face that
   mildly frowned.

Then a bubble of saliva sailed off down the helpless tongue
As quickly as you moved when skating on the ice when young,
A boy in Stafford's, with a good six of your decades still
   unsung.

A thought weighed heavy on us, the one word left unsaid.
Nurses swarmed and a screen was hurried about your bed.
Fact stung. No pulse. Heart beat. Dead beat. All over. Dead.

## STRAND DUMP AT IRISHTOWN

A blizzard of seagulls.
Wind belches in from the Irish Sea
That's acrid with assailing winter.
Garbage bellies out toward the frothy waves.
Earning a wage with Stone & Son, Ringsend
I drive into a mad-house of gulls,
Empty a Ford Transit of Swiftian rubble.
The yellow beaks are seething.
White craws are sufflated
With scourings and sweepings.

Cabbed against the lesser filthy storm
Of shit droppings, I'm loath to get out
Mingle with the swooping bickering gulls.
I've nothing in the way of offal, husks or crumbs
Fruit like the Dublin Corporation offers.
The attendant, clad in his important bright orange,
Waves me on toward the edge of the sea.

As I lurch forward across the debris of a capital,
An old tramp scavenges across my route to the foam.
A priest of middens, his tweeds are in rags.
His porcupine head is spiked to a contemptuous grey.
Clothes and the next supper play on his wits.
He holds up torn flowery panties to the breeze
And laughs and spits. As I swerve to pass,
He grills the functionless bric-a-brac of the outcast.
His cathechetical nose sniffs for edibles
Where Joyce once went walking into infinity.

As Corporation drivers empty their automatic lorries,
Depart to revictual through the December City,
Gulls sheer off my windscreen as in Hitchcock.
Having no tip-up, I must vacate the warm cab,
Taste on my tongue the busy rag-and-bone shore.
Marooned and dizzy among the crying sea-birds,

As the world wheels vertiginous with gold beaks,
I hear the pentecostal dismay of the heavens.
My lips have not flabbergasted the multitudes.
I petrify a little daily with Stone & Son.

I unload all my rubble with undue poignance.
At McFerrans and Dockrells I'm addressed as Stone.
Clambering back into the cab, I rev off a piece,
Where a lava of concrete spews down the rocks,
Halts the salt tide, I stop. It's lunch-break.
Downing my milk and rough round of honeyed bread,
I muse on the white crows of a young inland child:
These char-birds, raucous with appetite, intent
On spoilage. I empty them my crusts and dregs,
Watch a demise of dream froth the Viking Bay.

Sun streams in the cab window, fools with spring.
Lowering the glass, I'm hit with the stench,
This offertory of off-white crazy doves:
They shit and soar on delicate wings.
I envy the old rapparee on his altar,
Like him find a communion in the wild sky,
Where a cold and luminous storm is circling
With silvered bodies in a darkening unison.

# Paul Durcan

b. 1944

## PROTESTANT OLD FOLKS' COACH TOUR OF THE RING OF KERRY

Although it was a summer's day
It rained as though it was winter;
I pressed my nose against the windowpane,
The zoo-like windowpane of the coach,
And I closed my eyes and dreamed,
Dreamed that I was swimming,
Swimming in the coves of Kerry
With my young man Danny
And no one else about;
Danny, Danny, dripping wet,
Laughing through his teeth;
Blown to bits at Ypres.
Behind my eyes it is sunshine still
Although he has gone;
And my mother and father pad about the farm
Like ghosts cut out of cardboard;
When they died I too looked ghostly
But I stayed alive although I don't know how;
Dreaming to put the beehives back on their feet,
Waiting for Danny to come home.
And now I'm keeping house for brother Giles
Who stayed at home today to milk the cows;
Myself, I am a great jowled cow untended
And when I die I would like to die alone.

# THE DIFFICULTY THAT IS MARRIAGE

We disagree to disagree, we divide, we differ;
Yet each night as I lie in bed beside you
And you are faraway curled up in sleep
I array the moonlit ceiling with a mosaic of question-marks;
How was it I was so lucky to have ever met you?
I am no brave pagan proud of my mortality
Yet gladly on this changeling earth I should live for ever
If it were with you, my sleeping friend.
I have my troubles and I shall always have them
But I should rather live with you for ever
Than exchange my troubles for a changeless kingdom.
But I do not put you on a pedestal or throne;
You must have your faults but I do not see them.
If it were with you, I should live for ever.


# SHE MENDS AN ANCIENT WIRELESS

You never claimed to be someone special;
Sometimes you said you had no special talent;
Yet I have seen you rear two dancing daughters
With care and patience and love unstinted;
Reading or telling stories, knitting gansies
And all the while holding down a job
In the teeming city, morning until dusk.
And in the house when anything went wrong
You were the one who fixed it without fuss;
The electricity switch which was neither on nor off,
The t.v. aerial forever falling out;
And now as I watch you mend an ancient wireless
From my tiny perch I cry once more your praises
And call out your name across the great divide—Nessa.

## THE WEEPING HEADSTONES
## OF THE ISAAC BECKETTS

The Protestant graveyard was a forbidden place
So naturally as children we explored its precincts:
Clambered over drystone walls under elms and chestnuts,
Parted long grasses and weeds, poked about under yews,
Reconnoitred the chapel whose oak doors were always closed,
Stared at the schist headstones of the Isaac Becketts.
And then we would depart with mortal sins in our bones
As ineradicable as an arthritis
But we had seen enough to know what the old folks meant
When we would overhear them whisperingly at night refer to
"The headstones of the Becketts—they would make you
    weep."
These arthritises of sin:—
But although we had only six years each on our backs
We could decipher
Brand-new roads open up through heaven's fields
And upon them—like thousands upon thousands
Of people kneeling in the desert—
The weeping headstones of the Isaac Becketts.


## THE PROBLEM OF FORNICATION
## ON THE BLARNEY CHRONICLE

Yes—well I think that there is far too much fornication going
    on
At *The Blarney Chronicle*,
Particularly in the Reporters' Room,
And indeed the situation is as bad among the Sub-Editors;
I mean—it is one thing to have fornication in the Reporters'
    Room
But it seems to me quite another thing—quite another
    altogether
To have fornication going on to the same or even greater extent

Among the Sub-Editors; and that's not the end of it:
At teabreak this morning (actually I had coffee myself)
One of the Proof-Readers,
An extremely personable and sycophantic chap called
     Ermanaric Van Dal
(Yes, it *is* a name to play with, isn't it—Celtic I suppose—
Although it is rumoured that he is of Danish extraction
And I should not be surprised if that's the case)
Well, he told me that among the Proof-Readers
There is A Whole Lot of Fornicating Going On;
It sounds like the name of a pop song;
You simply cannot sustain or indeed tolerate fornication on
     that scale
On a newspaper—certainly not on a serious, low-quality
     newspaper
The likes of *The Blarney Chronicle*
And, as for the situation in the Typists' Pool, well I mean . . .
The only thing to do is to get hold of the Oxford English
     Dictionary
As well as of course one's own sexuality—
By the way, have you seen the report sent in by Field three
     hours ago
On the 28-year old Newry man shot dead in the head in front of
     his kiddies?
A Provisional I.R.A. show, of course;
Horse-Face Durcan wants to run a front-page story on this
But I've had to remind Horse-Face that there's no room on *The
     Blarney*
On the front page or any other page for this kind of tear-jerker;
It just doesn't jerk anyone's tears anymore;
The dead sod was a Protestant and, besides, unemployed—
As I was saying, we must get hold of the Oxford Dictionary
And look up the word Fornication and, if necessary,
Send for the Gárda Síochána or, at the very least,
Give the Attorney-General's office a buzz—you know the sort
     of bilge—
"Problem of Fornication in Blarney Castle!
Fornication: yes F-O-R-N (Forn) I-C-A-T-I-O-N (ication):
No: it's not *pub*lication—it's *forn*ication:

FORNICATION, fuck it."
Look: I know what: the best thing to do
Is for Gordon to write a Sermon on it
(After all there has not been a sermon-writer like Gordon
Since Thomas formulated in the abstract with his wife,
North-west of Anatolia, I think it was)
"Fornication In The Backyard"—sort of thing:
On the other hand, the female journalists in the union chapel
Are all militantly pro-fornication
So that if Gordon leans in an anti-fornication direction
There might well be more pants flying about the place than
    ever . . .
Frankly, Frank, I don't know what the shite to do:
Strange bag of tricks—fornication—isn't it?
They put that Newry bugger's brains in an envelope for his
    widow:
At least there is a streak of decency left in the world.


## THE PREGNANT PROPRIETRESS
## OF THE FISH AND CHIPPER


The pregnant proprietress of the fish and chipper
Is not the mother of God: but she is the mother of life
In the city of death: she has shed all beauty
And huge with child she plods in the sawdust
Wrapping the fishes, and scooping the chips.
She talks with her back to you; tiny but huge
In her stained blue coat and her frayed black slippers
And all the boys and the girls, the strays and the runaways,
Catching the fraction in the mathematics of talk.
She deals them out fivepences to play her favourite song
On the juke-box; "Play me *One-Man Band* by Leo Sayer."
But her own conversation is music—a one-woman symphony
In whose congenial forests boys and girls can rediscover
Their true monkey natures, their gibbon greatness.

# MEMOIRS OF A FALLEN BLACKBIRD

They liked me when I was on the wing
And I could whistle and I could sing;
But now that I am in my bed of clay
They come no more to be with me.

It was on the main road half-way between
Newcastle West and Abbeyfeale;
A juggernaut glanced me as it passed me by
And that was the end of the road for me.

Later that day, as I lay on the verge,
A thin rake of a young man picked me up
Into his trembling hands, and he stared
At me full quarter of an hour, he stared

At me and then he laid me down
And with his hands scooped me a shallow grave;
His soul passed into me as he covered me o'er;
I fear for him now where'er he be.

They liked me when I was on the wing
And I could whistle and I could sing;
But now that I am in my bed of clay
They come no more to be with me.

## MAKING LOVE OUTSIDE
## ÁRAS AN UACHTARÁIN

When I was a boy, myself and my girl
Used bicycle up to the Phoenix Park;
Outside the gates we used lie in the grass
Making love outside Áras An Uachtaráin.

Often I wondered what De Valera would have thought
Inside in his ivory tower
If he knew that we were in his green, green grass
Making love outside Áras An Uachtaráin.

Because the odd thing was—oh how odd it was—
We both revered Irish patriots
And we dreamed our dreams of a green, green flag
Making love outside Áras An Uachtaráin.

But even had our names been Diarmaid and Gráinne
We doubted De Valera's approval
For a poet's son and a judge's daughter
Making love outside Áras An Uachtaráin.

I see him now in the heat-haze of the day
Blindly stalking us down;
And, levelling an ancient rifle, he says "Stop
Making love outside Áras An Uachtaráin."

*Áras An Uachtaráin*: official residence of the President of Ireland. [ed.]

# THE MARRIED MAN WHO FELL IN LOVE WITH A SEMI-STATE BODY

Ted Rice was that abnormal creature—a normal man:
Merrily married, he was a good husband to his wife,
A good father to his children, and a friendly neighbour:
Until in the winter of 1964 he resigned his job
As manager of a centre-city pub to become
An executive with a Semi-State Body, Bord Ól,
In charge of the promotion of the Alcohol Industry.
So much did Ted Rice grow to love the Semi-State Body,
So hard he worked for her,
So heroically he hullaballoo'd for her,
So hopefully he hopped for her,
So heartily he hooted for her,
So harshly he harped for her,
So headlong he hunted for her,
That he began to think of her as The Woman In His Life
And one day as the train shot slowly down the line towards
    Cork
He had a vision of her as an American negress in a state of
    semi-undress
And, as such, he introduced her to the Cork Chamber of
    Commerce:
Even the most drunken members of his audience blinked
As Mr Rice introduced the invisible woman standing beside
    him;
And when, in the peroration of his speech, he fondled her
    breasts
Temperance men broke their pledges and ordered
    double brandies:
When Mr Rice departed for the railway station on the arm of
    his queen
He left behind him the Metropole Hotel strewn with bodies;
And half-way up the line he pulled the excommunication cord
And, introducing his Semi-State Body to the medieval ruins of
    a friary, declared:

"Let us sleep here together until the advertising boys
    arrive . . ."
Since then he has eked out the years in a mental hospital ward,
Tramping up and down the aisle of gloom in a shower of tears,
Repeating over and over: "I loved her, I loved her."


## THE DEATH BY HEROIN
## OF SID VICIOUS


There—but for the clutch of luck—go I.

At daybreak—in the arctic fog of a February daybreak—
Shoulderlength helmets in the watchtowers of the
    concentration camp
Caught me out in the intersecting arcs of the swirling
    searchlights:

There were at least a zillion of us caught out there
—Like ladybirds under a boulder—
But under the microscope each of us was unique.

Unique and we broke for cover, crazily breasting
The barbed wire and some of us made it
To the forest edge, but many of us did not

Make it, although their unborn children did—
Such as you whom the camp commandant branded
Sid Vicious of the Sex Pistols. Jesus, break his fall:

There—but for the clutch of luck—go we all.

*February 1979*

# Liam Murphy

b. 1948


## GOOD FRIDAY 1982

redundant
as easy to enunciate
as statistic

clean sheet cold
as inarticulate

no work to go to in the morning

nowhere to feel pain

retreat to the sea
timeless enough to heal
but careless enough to hurt

pain is in the explanation
as sun rehearses its easter dance

behind me the sandhills brood
as total as landmass to island

what's good about it
being redundant
stone separate in water

work pride as useless
as to walk on sparkling wave
easter egg surprise on your chin
rock bottom

water colder than it looks
in perpetual employment
crashing in ebbing out

rock bottom dropped out
humiliated by statistic
of forms and claims
and dates of birth of children

dependants
have I claimed before
in damp smoke-filled arena
queueing for entitlement

to what
to rock bottom
pay related
earned as I earned
when I earned

emasculated in the manpower office
of prospects
psychological hopes rocked
if only I were rock
not fish in ocean

and in the mornings
my children kiss me goodbye
as they set out
to birthright and the
wrongs of man.

# FOR FEAR OF WAKING
# THE ALARM CLOCK

when we married
        and came to live
                where i was born
she decided we'd sleep
        in my old nursery
and i was closer love
        than dinky toys
her happiness traced
        the wallpaper
of my dreams
mickey mouse and daffy duck
and our hearts beat
        like tin drums
together in a castle
with cavalry and indians
    soldiers and cannon guns
love
        and within her
i felt that she
had always been there
living behind the wallpaper
guiding the tenderness
        of days
until toys were tossed
        in a corner
and love played games
        with childhood dreams.

# Michael Davitt

b. 1950

## MEIRG AGUS LIOS LUACHRA

*do Mháire*

gur imigh an t-am
mar seo mar siúd
sall timpeall
faoi
gurbh é an t-am a d'imigh
an t-am a bhí romhainn
sa todhchaí
is go rabhamar
tráthnóna síoraí samhraidh
i reilig seanghluaisteán
ar fán
i measc fothraigh
na *model t's*
go raibh meirg ar do lámha
ar do ghúna fada bán
go rabhamar cosnocht
beo bocht
griandóite go cnámh
go rabhthas ag sméideadh orainn
trí fhuinneog traenach
a bhí ag filleadh
ó chraobh na héireann
i naoi déag tríocha ceathair
gur leanamar í tamall
feadh an iarnróid
gur fhilleamar abhaile
ar an gcoill rúnghlas
thíos ar ghrinneall locha
mar a raibh ár lios luachra
go raibh ceol mileoidin in uachtar

# RUST AND RAMPART OF RUSHES

*for Máire*

that time weaved
this way that way
over around
under
so that time past
was time before us
in the future
and that we were
one eternal summer evening
in a graveyard of old cars
wandering
among the ruins
of model t's
that there was rust on your hands
rust on your long white dress
that we were barefoot
penniless
sunburnt to the bone
that we were waved to
from the window of a train
returning from
the all-ireland final
in nineteen thirty four
that we followed it awhile
along the line
home
to our green and secret wood
down in the lake's bed
where our rampart of rushes stood
that it was all melodeon music

*mediums* pórtair á n-ól
arán tí ar bord
go raibh pearsana anaithnid
ina scáileanna ar snámh
idir sinn agus dán
go raibh bearnaí mistéireacha le dathú
agus véarsaí le cur lenár ngrá
sara mbeadh an pictiúr
iomlán


## SEANDAOINE

Chuimil sí a teanga dem shrón ghoirt
is dem spéaclaí a bhí sioctha
ag an sáile cáite is d'iarr sí orm
na luibheanna a ainmniú. A ainmniú?
(ní aithneoinnse an chopóg ón neantóg
an dtuigeann tú.)
Bhuel stathamar an crobh préacháin
is an méaracán dearg (an Dálach
a d'ainmnigh ar ball iad
á choisreacan féin faoi thrí)
is dúrtsa gur sheandaoine iad
a léimeadh isteach sa chlaí
chun beannú do na gluaisteáin
is go rabhadar ag beannú dúinne
anois ar dhá thaobh an chasáin.
Leagamar síos ar thinteán an Dálaigh iad
gur eachtraigh sé dúinn mar a bhris
Peig Sayers a cromán lá dár thug
bean leighis lán a croibh
de mhéiríní sí isteach sa tigh chuici.
Nuair a d'fhilleamar abhaile
chuireamar ár bpiseoga faoi uisce
is chuireamar ar salann ár gcuimhne
tráthnóna lusach.

porter by the medium
home-made bread on the table
that unknown persons
were shadows floating
between us and fate
that there were gaps of mystery to be painted
and verses to be added to our love
before the picture be
complete

*translated by Gabriel Rosenstock and Michael Hartnett*

## OLD PEOPLE

She licked my salty nose
and my glasses which were frosted
by the sea spray and she asked me
to name the plants. Me name plants?
(I couldn't tell a dock from a nettle
you know.)
Well, we pulled the crowsfoot
and foxglove (Daly
named them for us later
crossing himself three times)
and I said these were old people
who had jumped into the hedge
to salute the motorcars
and were saluting us now
from both sides of the pathway.
We laid them down on Daly's fireplace
and he related to us
that Peig Sayers broke her hip one day
after a healing woman had brought her
a handful of foxgloves unannounced.
When we got home
we put our superstitions in water
and preserved in salt the memory
of a herbal afternoon.

*translated by Michael Hartnett and Michael Davitt*

## I gCUIMHNE AR LÍS CEÁRNAIGHE, BLASCAODACH (†1974)

Tráth bhíodh cártaí ar bord,
Coróin is mugaí tae faoi choinneal
Cois tine ar caorthainn;
Asal amuigh san oíche,
Madraí tamall gan bhia
Is seanbhean dom mharú le Gaolainn.

Tráth bhíodh an chaint tar éis Aifrinn
Is nárbh í a dhamnaigh faisean
Stróinséirí in aon fhéachaint shearbhasach amháin
Is nár chuir sí Laethanta Breátha
Ó Ollscoil Chorcaí ina n-áit:
"An tuairgín", "an coca féir", "an fuaisceán."

Tráth prátaí is maicréal
Le linn na nuachta i lár an lae
Ba mhinic a fiafraí
Mar nár fhlúirseach a cuid Béarla
Is déarfainn dhera go rabhadar ag marú a chéile
I dtuaisceart na hÉireann.

Tráth bhíodh sí ina dealbh
Ag fuinneog bharr an staighre
Ar strae siar amach thar ché
Abhaile chun an oileáin i dtaibhreamh
Is dá dtiocfainn suas de phreib taobh thiar di:
"Ó mhuise fán fad' ort, a chladhaire."

## IN MEMORY OF ELIZABETH KEARNEY, BLASKETISLANDER (†1974)

Once it was cards on the table,
Rosary and mugs of tea in candlelight
Beside a blazing fire;
Outside, a donkey in the night,
Dogs denied their diet
And an old woman destroying me with Irish.

Once, there was the after-Mass chatting,
And she would trim the sails
Of strangers with one caustic look of her eye
Putting the College Trippers
Firmly in their places
With "pestles" and "hencrabs" and "haycocks"!

Once, at mackerel and potatoes
During the news at noon-time
She'd ask for a translation
Because her English was lacking
And I'd say: "Yera they're killing each other
In the North of Ireland."

Once, she was like a statue
At the top-stairs window
Wandering west from the quayside
Home in a dream to her island
And if I suddenly came up behind her
She'd say: "Oh, you thief, may you long be homeless!"

*translated by Michael Hartnett and Michael Davitt*

## AN SCÁTHÁN

*i gcuimhne m'athar*

I

Níorbh é m'athair níos mó é
ach ba mise a mhacsan;
paradacsa fuar a d'fháisceas,
dealbh i gculaith Dhomhnaigh
a cuireadh an lá dár gcionn.

Dhein sé an-lá deora, seirí,
fuiscí, ceapairí feola is tae.
Bhí seanchara leis ag eachtraí
faoi sciurd lae a thugadar
ar Eochaill sna triochaidí
is gurbh é a chéad pháirtí é
i seirbhís Chorcaí/An Sciobairín
amach sna daicheadaí.
Bhí dornán cártaí Aifrinn
ar mhatal an tseomra suí
ina gcorrán thart ar vás gloine,
a bhronntanas scoir ó C.I.E.

II

Níorbh eol dom go ceann dhá lá
gurbh é an scáthán a mharaigh é ...

An seanscáthán ollmhór Victeoiriach
leis an bhfráma ornáideach bréagórga
a bhí romhainn sa tigh trí stór
nuair a bhogamar isteach ón tuath.
Bhínn scanraithe roimhe: go sciorrfadh
anuas den bhfalla is go slogfadh mé
d'aon tromanáil i lár na hoíche ...

Ag maisiú an tseomra chodlata dó
d'ardaigh sé an scáthán anuas

# THE MIRROR

*in memory of my father*

I

He was no longer my father
but I was still his son;
I would get to grips with that cold paradox,
the remote figure in his Sunday best
who was buried the next day.

A great day for tears, snifters of sherry,
whiskey, beef sandwiches, tea.
An old mate of his was recounting
their day excursion
to Youghal in the Thirties,
how he was his first partner
on the Cork/Skibbereen route
in the late Forties.
There was a splay of Mass cards
on the sitting-room mantelpiece
which formed a crescent round a glass vase,
his retirement present from C.I.E.

II

I didn't realise till two days later
it was the mirror took his breath away.

The monstrous old Victorian mirror
with the ornate gilt frame
we had found in the three-storey house
when we moved in from the country.
I was afraid that it would sneak
down from the wall and swallow me up
in one gulp in the middle of the night.

While he was decorating the bedroom
he had taken down the mirror

gan lámh chúnta a iarraidh;
ar ball d'iompaigh dath na cré air,
an oíche sin phléasc a chroí.


III

Mar a chuirfí de gheasa orm
thugas faoin jab a chríochnú:
an folús macallach a pháipéarú,
an fhuinneog ard a phéinteáil,
an doras marbhlainne
a scríobadh. Nuair a rugas ar an scáthán
sceimhlíos. Bhraitheas é ag análú tríd.
Chuala é ag rá i gcogar téiglí:
*I'll give you a hand, here.*

Is d'ardaíomar an scáthán thar n-ais in airde
os cionn an tinteáin,
m'athair á choinneáil
fad a dheineas-sa é a dhaingniú
le dhá thairne.

without asking for help;
soon he turned the colour of terracotta
and his heart broke that night.


III

There was nothing for it
but to set about finishing the job,
papering over the cracks,
painting the high window,
stripping the door, like the door of a crypt.
When I took hold of the mirror
I had a fright. I imagined him breathing through it.
I heard him say in a reassuring whisper:
*I'll give you a hand, here.*

And we lifted the mirror back in position
above the fireplace,
my father holding it steady
while I drove home
the two nails.

*translated by Paul Muldoon*

# Gregory O'Donoghue

b. 1951

## MATHEMATICIAN

The smell of sweet wood,
your yellowed skin, neck

thin as a turkey's gizzard—
and now we bump you down

to rest not even on
the ruins of relatives;

though I doubt that
makes a difference—

I need to suppose
loneliness like your meticulous

work must cease, your urge
to take even minor matters

to their square root—
I know you filed love letters—

& perhaps you would approve
this sense of things wrapped up,

mourners, a ring—
not to group around you again.

## SECRET BLESSING

Against whatever nightmare
Made you whimper, against
The cranking and humming of
The sinister quays—a weak
Friend so often, I hold you.
The moon through the window finds
Something strangely saddening
Along the blur of your cheek.
It was never there before.
In secret blessing I slip
A slight kiss along your forehead,
Waiting for your breathing
To settle; although you are
Stronger in your way than I,
Tonight you are in my care.

## GLOBE

*for Robert Perkins*

All clocks stopped,
Again I cannot tell
What room this is;
I am dreaming at

The core of a globe—
A sea urchin world—
Of a spectral moon
Over tall orchards:

I inhabit tonight
A world of uncertain
Odd sensations, a randomness
I have come to trust.

Pale as limbs, moonlight
Descends through a top hole—
Moving to sit
Where an orange kitten

Curls like a prawn.
And slowly, while I still
Smell fur, rich urchin roe,
The moon raises her baton

And one by one brass and
Woodwind rise, dusty from
Their plots, yellow
As long buried bone,

And one by one
They are chanting goodbye
Before they take their
Hundred instruments up:

A random and seemingly
Senseless world in which
I must come to trust again,
And again, and again.


## THE GLASS


Something long ago had snapped
and nailed him to a high bar stool.
Whatever he might reason, useless!
Logic alone can never act.

A riddle to the end;
listen to its silence.
Now and then something like a caress,
a throbbing in the glass. . . .

We tell his tale in metaphors:
that one July a baby hedgehog fell
alive in the emptied pond; flies laid
eggs to hatch in the midday sun

& for hours after
the white maggots bored, and fed.
Forever, humming:

it would be good to start again
in another country; it would be good
for once not to drink the fare.
And something in the eye of a friend

tells him again that somewhere
along the line he went too far.


## A NOMAD

Imagine a man
Who has mastered, along
With foreign currencies,
The inoffensive smirk.

Who comes and goes
As though he belonged;
As if to say that in
Any back-of-the-beyond

He is at least
As matter-of-fact as
Ticking red lights
Descending on runways.

He might never have imagined
Endless notes in bottles,
Or dreamed that love
Or some other miracle

Could tell him who he is:
On a picnic-chair,
At a lake's edge, a thin
Man with an open map.


## ANNA AKHMATOVA

*after her* Requiem

Another anniversary; I hear you
Dragged to the window, your dead

Heels across the floorboards;
Again you shake your beautiful head

And say: "Coming here is coming home."
I can't remember all their names,

The marvellous books are burned:
For them I have stitched a wide shroud

From their own words; I will never
Forget them, even if my mouth is broken.

Do not build a memorial to me
Near the sea where I was born;

Nor in Tsarsky Sad by the sacred stump
Where an inconsolate ghost calls me;

Build it here by the bolted door
That even in death I will remember

The horror of the Black Marias;
Here where an old woman yelped

Like a kicked pup—let the snow thaw
In streams from my bronze eyelids,

Let the prison dove call,
And the boats go quietly in the mist.


# AQUARIUM

*I am a man upon the land*
*I am a Selkie in the sea.*    (TRAD.)

I build a minute world
Of filters, coloured rocks
And long fern weeds
For guppies, minnowy swordtails

The ink dark molly;
I clean it for the angels
Who on fanned fins and threads
Glide awed mucous mouths

To procreate in a kiss:
Creation stilled to an eye
Seasonless Paradiso
The great fish summoned at will

Or dismissed—Ahab's
Breeching monster!
And remember at ease
Boston's great cylinder

Of wistful eels
Blunt snookered sharks
Gliding back from the glass;
By the sway of the moray

I conjured the green scales
Of a selkie at the chapel door
And heard desire return
In cries, the keen of seals.

# Nuala Ní Dhomhnaill

b. 1952

## LEABA SHÍODA

Do chóireoinn leaba duit
i Leaba Shíoda
sa bhféar ard
faoi iomrascáil na gcrann
is bheadh do chraiceann ann
mar shíoda ar shíoda
sa doircheacht
am lonnaithe na leamhan.

Craiceann a shníonn
go gléineach thar do ghéaga
mar bhainne á dháil as crúiscíní
am lóin
is tréad gabhar ag gabháil thar chnocáin
do chuid gruaige
cnocáin ar a bhfuil faillte arda
is dhá ghleann atá domhain.

Is bheadh do bheola taise
ar mhilseacht shiúcra
tráthnóna is sinn ag spaisteoireacht
cois abhann
is na gaotha meala
ag séideadh thar an Sionna
is na fiúisí ag beannú duit
ceann ar cheann.

Na fiúisí ag ísliú
a gceanna maorga
ag umhlú síos don áilleacht

## LABASHEEDY (THE SILKEN BED)

I'd make a bed for you
in Labasheedy
in the tall grass
under the wrestling trees
where your skin
would be silk upon silk
in the darkness
when the moths are coming down.

Skin which glistens
shining over your limbs
like milk being poured
from jugs at dinnertime;
your hair is a herd of goats
moving over rolling hills,
hills that have high cliffs
and two ravines.

And your damp lips
would be as sweet as sugar
at evening and we walking
by the riverside
with honeyed breezes
blowing over the Shannon
and the fuchsias bowing down to you
one by one.

The fuchsias bending low
their solemn heads
in obeisance to the beauty

os a gcomhair
is do phriocfainn péire acu
mar shiogairlíní
is do mhaiseoinn do chluasa
mar bhrídeog.

Ó, chóireoinn leaba duit
i Leaba Shíoda
le hamhascarnach an lae
i ndeireadh thall
is ba mhór an pléisiúr dúinn
bheith géaga ar ghéaga
ag iomrascáil
am lonnaithe na leamhan.


## MÓR GORAÍ


Táimse á rá leat,
A Mhóir mhí-choibhseach,
go dtiocfaidh naithreacha uaithne
amach as do bholg
má fhanann tú ar gor
ar nimh na haithne
lá níos faide.

Cnuasaigh chugat isteach
mar bheach
na huaireanta cloig a osclaíonn amach
fén ngréin rinn-ghathach;
aibíonn siad sa teas.
Bailigh iad
is dein díobh
laetha meala.

in front of them
I would pick a pair of flowers
as pendant earrings
to adorn you
like a bride in shining clothes.

O I'd make a bed for you
in Labasheedy,
in the twilight hour
with evening falling slow
and what a pleasure it would be
to have our limbs entwine
wrestling
while the moths are coming down.


## MÓR HATCHING

I'm telling you
stubborn Mór,
that green snakes will come
out of your womb
if you stay sitting
on festering knowledge
one day longer.

Gather into yourself
like a bee
the hours that fall open
under the bright shaft of the sun
ripening in heat.
Store them
and make of them
days of honey.


*Mór*: earth/mother goddess associated with the Dingle
    peninsula [ed.]

# I mBAILE AN tSLÉIBHE

I mBaile an tSléibhe
tá Cathair Léith
is laistíos dó
tigh mhuintir Dhuinnshléibhe;
as san chuaigh an file Seán
'on Oileán
is uaidh sin tháinig an ghruaig rua
is bua na filíochta
anuas chugam
trí cheithre ghlún.

Ar thaobh an bhóthair
tá seidhleán
folaithe ag crainn fiúise,
is an feileastram
buí
ó dheireadh mhí Aibreáin
go lár an Mheithimh,
is sa chlós tá boladh
lus anainne nó camán meall
mar a thugtar air sa dúiche
timpeall,
i gCill Uru is i gCom an Liaigh
i mBaile an Chóta is i gCathair Boilg.

Is lá
i gCathair Léith
do léim breac geal
ón abhainn
isteach sa bhuicéad
ar bhean
a chuaigh le ba
chun uisce ann,
an tráth
gur sheoil trí árthach
isteach sa chuan,

## IN BAILE AN tSLÉIBHE

In Baile an tSléibhe
is Cathair Léith
and below it
the house of the Dunleavies;
from here the poet Seán
went into the Great Blasket
and from here the red hair
and gift of poetry came down to me
through four generations.

Beside the road
there is a stream
covered over with fuchsias
and the wild flag
yellow
from the end of April
to mid-June,
and in the yard there is a scent
of pineapple mayweed or camomile
as it is commonly known in the surrounding countryside,
in Cill Uru and in Coumaleague
in Ballincota and in Caherbullig.

And one day
in Cathair Léith
a white trout leapt
out of the river
and into the bucket
of a woman
who had led her cows
to water there;
a time
when three ships came sailing
into the bay

gur neadaigh an fiolar
i mbarr an chnoic
is go raibh laincisí síoda
faoi chaoire na Cathrach.

## NA SÚILE UAINE

Sular ghliúc
súile uaine
an nathar nimhe
san uaigneas

bhí rincí fada Andalúiseacha
cíortha cnáimh
is gúnaí tafata
ag déanamh glóir
mar thor cabáiste
sular ghliúc na súile uaine.

Sular lúb sé
lúb na lúibe
síos ar bhrainse
na n-úll cumhra

bhí hataí péacacha
faoi chleití piasún
is bataí droighin
faoi lámhchrainn éabhair
bhí cailí láis
is drithliú ar éadach
sular lúb sé síos ar ghéag ann.

Sular ith sé
greim den úll ann
bhí cnaipí ag oscailt
i ndiaidh a chéile
bhí cabhail á nochtadh

the eagle was still nesting
on the top of the hill
and the sheep of Cathair
had spancels of silk.


## THE GREEN EYES

Before the green eyes
of the serpent
gleamed
in the wilderness

there were long Andalusian dances
combs of bone
and dresses of taffeta
making swishing sounds
like leaves of cabbage
before the green eyes gleamed.

Before he looped
the loop of the loop
down the sweet-scented apple-branch

there were jaunty hats
with pheasant feathers
blackthorn sticks
with tops of ivory,
veils of lace
and shimmering dresses
before he looped along the branch there.

Before he took
a bite of the apple
there were buttons being opened
one after another
bodies being unclothed

faoi scáilí oíche
bhí gruaig rua
ar gach lánún ann
is iad ag péinteáil breicní
ar a chéile
le gathanna gréine;
ag mionghairí
sular bhain sé greim den úll ann.

Ach anois
tá an greim bainte
an t-úll ite
an chnuimh ginte
ár gcosa nite
is taimid luite
sa dorchadas síorraí
mar a bhfuil gol is gárthaíl
is díoscán fiacal
go heireaball timpeall.


VENIO EX ORIENTE

Tugaim liom spíosraí an Oirthir
is rúin na mbasár
is cúmhráin na hAráibe
ná gealfaidh do láimhín bán.

Tá henna i m'chuid ghruaige
is péarlaí ar mo bhráid
is tá cróca meala na bhfothach
faoi cheilt i m'imleacán.

Ach tá mus eile ar mo cholainnse,
boladh na meala ó Imleach Shlat
go mbíonn blas mísmín is móna uirthi
is gur dorcha a dath.

in night-shadows,
every couple was red-haired
and busily painting freckles
on each other
with shafts of sunlight
laughingly,
before he took a bite of the apple.

But now
the bite is bitten
the apple is eaten
the maggot begotten
our feet finally bathed
and we are lying
in the eternal darkness
where there is crying and wailing
and gnashing of teeth
in saeculorum.

*translations by the author*


## VENIO EX ORIENTE

Eastern spices I bring with me,
and from bazaars, a mystery:
and perfumes from Arabic land
would not make bright your small white hand.

My hair is henna-brown
and pearls from my neck hang down
and my navel here conceals
vials of the honey of wild bees.

But my body breathes another musk
that smells of wild mint and turf:
scent of honey from an ancient hill
that has darkness in its tint.

## NÍ FÉIDIR LIOM LUÍ ANSEO NÍOS MÓ

Ní féidir liom luí anseo níos mó
i do bholadh
tú béal faoi ar an bpiliúr
i do chodladh
do lámh go neafuiseach
thar mo chromán
faoi mar ba chuma leat sa deireadh
mé bheith as nó ann.

Ní hé d'easpa suime
a chuireann orm
ná cuimhní samhraidh aoibhinn
ag briseadh tharam
ní hé an próca bláth ag barr na leapa
a chuireann ar meisce mé
ach boladh do cholainne,
meascán fola is cré.

Éireod as an leaba
is cuirfead orm.
Goidfead do chuid eochracha
as do dhorn
is tiománfad chun na cathrach.
Amárach ar a naoi
gheobhair glaoch gutháin
á rá cár féidir leat dul
ag triall ar do ghluaisteán

ach ní féidir liom luí anseo níos mó
i do bholadh
nó titfidh mé i ngrá leat, b'fhéidir.

# I CANNOT LIE HERE ANYMORE ...

I cannot lie here anymore
in your aroma—
with your pillowed mouth
asnore,
your idle hand
across my hip
not really caring
whether I exist.

I'm not upset
because you ignore me
nor because our happy summer
washes over me—
it's not the bedside flowers
that intoxicate
but your body, your aroma,
a blend of blood and earth.

I'll get up from the bed
and put on my clothes
and leave with the carkeys
from your fist stolen
and drive to the city.

At nine tomorrow
you'll get a call
telling you where to go
to pick up your car—
but I cannot lie here anymore
where your aroma laps—
because I'll fall in love with you,
(perhaps)

*translations by Michael Hartnett*

# Aidan Murphy

b. 1952

## ELEGY FOR A BRIDE

*for Pauline*

Alive your preference was laughter.
You ran from the voice at the top of the stairs,
from the shadow of the huge hands &
the drunken eye forever on the warpath.
Violence shot you with ice, made
nerves jump out of you like springs.
You ran for love, for someone who would
silence the castanets in your mouth.

When I think of you I am a wad of wool
spun coarsely on a stick, numb with novocaine.
Twelve impressionable years like mother & son
& now, an invisible wall even when I dream
(I follow you across a field but you float
away through a gap in a hedge I can't find
& I'm left staring at a bull, a barrier of leaves).

Death has changed you into an enigma.
Is it dark down there? Can you cope?
Are you still running desperate for light?
Is the dream attempting contact? but how can I
replace your suffering with peace when I'm
stopped by the bull & the leaves & the wall
of living. No place to intersect.

But perhaps the drama is ended
& this unfeeling cold I sense
is the little shadow of annihilation?
Surely you deserve that twig of mercy?

# FRIENDSHIP

You know the painting I mean

two naked men stretched between
heaven & earth's brilliant extremes

veins & muscles straining
to link limbs. It continues
beyond the frame; the bodies writhe
struggling to cancel struggle,
to be whole and single.

But who gets to make the breakfast?
Who gets the much-needed rest?
And round two breaks
whose bloody heart?

                    Still
it is a free-for-all
and when you see something you want
you climb up on his shoulders.

Or one serene night in the shrubbery
he reveals himself, & you reassure
his hand before the door closes.

And tomorrow you break your heart
trying to remind him.

## MEMORIAL ALBERT CAMUS

He was a tenant here. A gentleman.
You'd hardly hear his footsteps on the boards.
He sat for hours on the balcony
sniffing night, savouring the cries of girls.

Ocean was his sabbath.
While he glided like a flatfish over
underwater orchards
we sweated in our pews, our ears
conches loud with death.

I controlled two dozen keys. I woke
one night & heard him frying eggs at four a.m.
Slept well last night monsieur? No answer.
I speak to all my guests as if on tape.

Sometimes I dream his body
hanging in my wardrobe, I unhook & wear.
In every cell of it a dolphin
whistles & a heart hopes.
I wake up stripped,
another day of orphaned colour.

## WHISTLING

The man going home alone
stares intentionally at nothing
and whistles. In bed I hear
his song of concentrated terror,
the tension of controlled breath.
It is a million years ago;
axe in hand he wades in slime,
slugs bubble at his knees.
Somewhere in the wet forest
another advances—a perfect
double, his own armed
cautious image, whistling
as he whistles, notes of fear.

Is this what music is, this
gentle Schumann spinning here
snowing on the world? Is it
born of an old reluctance
a turning from silence & self?
I feel relieved. The symphony
is over, & the man? The street
is empty, his tune gone.
Under the sheets I watch
lights fencing with the dark.
Pins are dropping on the quilt,
I purse my lips & blow.

# Maurice Riordan

b. 1953

## THE DRIFT

A wet night shelters the eels:
they slip downstream
through drenched grass; cross
meadows, ditches; coil into pools.

As a child I stoned one,
stilled it—a thing
recalled this night
entering again your otherness;

and a troupe of frogs
jumping like clowns
across a road, sequined
in the cone of a headlight;

sliced or crushed in their caper
through the farms; eels seeking
the Sargasso, melting into ocean,
cheated by continental drift:

a luminous mime, we drop
below the moon; each self
in an envelope of wet
plumbing sleep . . .

amphibious shapes converge.

## PURSUIT

Still I see you—
white upturned face, small
in a man's dufflecoat;

in how many stations
have you stood, stood & wavered,
stray flake in sleety rain.

# Thomas McCarthy

b. 1954

## STATE FUNERAL

> *Parnell will never come again, he said. He's there,*
> *all that was mortal of him. Peace to his ashes.*
> JAMES JOYCE, *Ulysses*

That August afternoon the family
Gathered. There was a native *déjà vu*
Of Funeral when we settled against the couch
On our sunburnt knees. We gripped mugs of tea
Tightly and soaked the TV spectacle;
The boxed ritual in our living-room.

My father recited prayers of memory,
Of monster meetings, blazing tar-barrels
Planted outside Free-State homes, the Broy-
Harriers pushing through a crowd, Blueshirts;
And, after the war, De Valera's words
Making Churchill's imperial palette blur.

What I remember is one decade of darkness,
A mind-stifling boredom; long summers
For blackberry picking and churning cream,
Winters for saving timber or setting lines
And snares: none of the joys of here and now
With its instant jam, instant heat and cream:

It was a landscape for old men. Today
They lowered the tallest one, tidied him
Away while his people watched quietly.
In the end he had retreated to the first dream,
Caning truth. I think of his austere grandeur;
Taut sadness, like old heroes he had imagined.

# DAEDALUS, THE MAKER

*for Seán Lucy*

Dactylos was silent and impersonal;
hidden behind false names, he achieved
a powerful *persona*. There was only
his work; a chipping of rock into form
and the rhythmic riveting of bronze,
diminishing his need for company.

Learning to keep silent is a difficult
task. To place Art anonymously at
the Earth's altar, then to scurry away
like a wounded animal, is the most cruel
test-piece. A proud maker, I have waited at
the temple doors for praise and argument.

Often I have abandoned an emerging form
to argue with priests and poets—
only to learn the wisdom of Dactylos:
that words make the strangest labyrinth,
with circular passages and minotaurs
lurking in the most innocent lines.

I will banish argument to work again
with bronze. Words, I have found, are
captured, not made: opinion alone is
a kind of retreat. I shall become like
Dactylos, a quiet maker; moving between
poet and priest, keeping my pride secret.

## THE RAREST THYME

For you I would have built a herb-garden,
Not a pathetic patch for mint and chives

But a real olitory, with old-
Fashioned southernwood and rarest thyme.

I might have built a wooden seat between
Two plants of rosemary, their astringent

Scent seeping through your workshirt to the clean
Flesh of your back. I would have grown a plant

Of basil for you to stroke into form;
And, certainly, a row of lavender

To infuse carefully over a warm
Stove, for you to sip at whenever

The world became darkened with sick headaches,
Or a loss of blood whitened your small hands.


## THE SORROW GARDEN

### I    HOLE, SNOW

It is an image of irreversible loss,
This hole in my father's grave that needs
Continuous filling. Monthly now, my
Uncle comes to shovel a heap of earth
From the spare mound. Tear-filled, he
Compensates the collapse of his brother's
Frame. I arrived on my motor-bike to help
But he will not share the weight of grief.

It is six months since my father's death
And he has had to endure a deep snow;
All night it came down, silently like time,
Smoothing everything into sameness. I
Visited the winter-cold grave, expecting
A set of his footprints, a snow-miracle.


## II    SMALL BIRDS, VOICES

These are the neatly twisted sounds of death,
Those small brown birds singing, small winter
Birds clinging to an overhanging bough.
Never in life did I know him to stare
So silence-stricken for one brief moment.

These birds recall the voices of his life:
A low cold note is the voice of torment
From childhood poverty and the brief, light
Notes are the tones of Love and Marriage.

"There's the beginning of *your* life's troubles",
A neighbour said at his grave. I arranged
The wilting wreath-flowers, feigning numbness.
Something, perhaps his voice, told me even then
How much of Love, Sorrow, Love one life contains.


## III    MISTING-OVER

These bright evenings I ride
through the young plantation
by the river; at times I can
see the young trees clearly
through the collapsing mist.

Sometimes in the misted river
at dusk his face at my left
shoulder has become distinctly
settled and lined with peace.

But now in the clouded pools
I drive through on the avenue,
he no longer calls out as if
injured by my rear wheel, but
is happy as clay, roads, memory.


IV   LOST WORDS, SORROWS

It's difficult to believe that it could
go on; this wanting to participate
in a rigid plan of water and wood,
words and wood and other inanimate
worlds that cannot explain sorrow.

Around me I find the forms that know
his lack of living. The wooden sculpture
on a shelf points to its lack of finish,
calls for a finishing touch, for his sure
and solid polish. I pray for its wish.

As if water could explain my crying,
I visited the salmon-weir after
a snow-fall. The fish were manoeuvring
through the spray, determined to get over
protective obstacles of wood and stone.

Like salmon through water, like virgin wood
disturbed into its form in art, his death
obfuscates words irrecoverably. Death plays
its own tune of vision and shadow. It has
attached itself as a vocabulary of change.

# HER WIDOWHOOD

*Ba mhaith liom triall go deireadh lae go brónach** 
SEÁN Ó RÍORDÁIN

A shaft of wind cuts through the wet garden,
Daffodils are forced to their full shower
Of yellowness. The tall azara that smelled
Of chocolate has sprung to life once more
Though its bark was cut, its bole half sawn.
Something of the old regeneration has left
Me: birds seem quiet, the furrows less clear.
The accuracy of new growth that blessed
Love's wandering eyes at our first sowing
Seems non-existent in the huge quietness
Left by his death. Plants revolt in my head—
This widowhood is like a nettle sting,
Blotching one's whole body with its whiteness,
Filling limbs and seed with the ache of the dead.

* see page 45

# THE PROVINCIAL WRITER'S DIARY

On cold nights in November he read late
and worried about the gift of fiction;
he was enveloped in a shell of lethargy.
Everything was let go—
even his diary lay idle for a whole month
while he chased provincial loneliness
from the corners of his mother's house.

Everything became consumed by the Personal:
furious theatre work killed some time,
strolling with his bachelor friends, fishing,
or the steady cumulative ritual of walking

beyond the city to sketch its grey limits.
But nowhere could he find (within those limits
of thought) the zeal that would consume life.

He lived far from the heroic. On Monday
mornings he would stalk the grey ghettos
of the North side and low-lying tenements
for absentee school-children. He would be taken aback
by the oppressive stench and filth of their lives.
One morning he thought, as if explaining all misery,
that such homes were the nests of the Military.


## PARTY SHRINE

*Come back,*
*Poor Twenty-Sixer. Live on lack.*
AUSTIN CLARKE


My father is clearing the first Party shrine:
it is the summer of Sixty-Six.
He hates physical work and everything
that keeps him from the protection racket
of crosswords and history books.
But the rest of the Committee
has been drunk since the Jubilee
and can't break the spell of itself.

Weeds know nothing about the Party
or how it emerged, genie-like,
out of an abandoned shell case.
The weeds and their friends the shitting
pigeons want to bury this shrine
in a single summer.
I am holding the shovel for my father
while he reads inscriptions on brass:
sixteen golden names of the Party,
the twenty-six grammatical flaws.

# ANDRÉ GIDE

At La Roque the swallows called, whirling round
the house, their tight marine cries piercing air
like words cut into black marble. I remember
their broods on a fine day, the fluffy sonar sound;
and Marie standing still in a blaze of sunlight,
daisies in her hand; and her loud purr at night,
the creak of her sex-life that pushed me from sleep
into the nocturnal business of the adult world.

Our Anna Shackleton was never disturbed at night
except to find the holiest way to die. Kindness
and beauty and upright posture couldn't compensate
for her poverty. I was the only male to undress
her days with care. Wanting nothing but her time,
I consumed her love like a liquorice; the two of us
lived at my herbarium, urging things to their prime.

Once, charged with Anna's love of growth, I took
a wounded starling from the grass, before the cats
shared its death. I felt that it had fallen from its
nest like an idea escaped from sentences. It shook
its mild beak and nested in my hands to pour scorn
on the idle cats. But when burdened with the earthworm
of my thought it flew back to its fields of corn.

Other starlings gathered in a warmer place. Athman
and Meriem, with their rich Mediterranean walk,
shoved spices in my face. Meriem dropped her *haik*
at the door one night to cure my tubercular limbs
with a firm and amber skin. But Athman I remember
best, weeping as my train left the oasis. Through him
the desert wept to see me going North to thought.

# Dennis O'Driscoll

b. 1954

## DEPARTURES

### I

Grain from the barn of memory.

You were the long churn of a lily,
the spilt milk of love.

### II   AFTER VINOKUROV

Objects speak louder than words.

And here is the stone that made the river dance.
Here is the gate that opened to friends once.

### III

Glass coffin of an airport has consumed you.

Your jet ploughs sky.
Its wings, like fingers, lift you out of reach.

## VILLAGE

*for George Mackay Brown*

sea lathers a scalp of rock
white fringes of deep waves toss

blackberry thimbles dangle from a needled bush
smoked cod, like varnished planks, hang in a shed

the small football stadium is a deserted amphitheatre
the telephone in its red kiosk rings and rings

hazy mountains are outlined like isotherms
noon airways broadcast peace

no shoppers, fishermen, schoolchildren in sight
no dog stretched under the wave-curling sun

no watercoloured jellyfish like melting ice
no bird flock shimmers on a wash of sky

and a petrified silence settles
like the pause after the whale,

its tail shaped like pleading arms,
is sucked into digestive juices of the sea

in craft shops built of oatmeal stone
kilns are warm still

on the roofless forge a tattered poster blows
its message, 'NO URANIUM', still partly legible


## SOMEONE

someone is dressing up for death today, a change of skirt or tie
eating a last feast of buttered sliced pan, tea
scarcely having noticed the erection that was his last
shaving his face to marble for the icy laying-out
spraying with deodorant her coarse armpit grass
someone today is leaving home on business
saluting, terminally, the neighbours who will join in the cortège
someone is trimming his nails for the last time, a precious
      moment
someone's thighs will not be streaked with elastic in the future
someone is putting out milkbottles for a day that will not come

someone's fresh breath is about to be taken clean away
someone is writing a cheque that will be marked 'drawer
   deceased'
someone is circling posthumous dates on a calendar
someone is listening to an irrelevant weather forecast
someone is making rash promises to friends
someone's coffin is being sanded, laminated, shined
who feels this morning quite as well as ever
someone if asked would find nothing remarkable in today's
   date
perfume and goodbyes her final will and testament
someone today is seeing the world for the last time
as innocently as he had seen it first


## BEING

*for Julie*


### I    CONCEPTION

juice of being is squeezed from a ripe body
craving with orgasmic joy for life
its bean sprouts hanging by a thread
to dreams of soccer leagues, investment bonds, mince pies

past chiffon folds of mucus
a spoon of sperm cracks open a moon egg
buries a head in its sand
finds its atmosphere habitable

a fossil brands the womb now
the prehistoric zip of spine, the lizard tail
the hard imprint of bone
frozen in molten fluids

in the opening scene
a couple walked the strand
a child's first cry will be
the sadness they feel after coition

## II ENTROPY

from the womb everything appeared beautiful
he swam, a goldfish, in the plastic water bag
peering with big eyes
behind the flimsy curtain,

a swollen bubble he longed to pierce:
but now the dented head
becomes a heavy globe
balanced on tilting axis of spine

his nerves, high-tension wires,
bear messages of fear
it is not enough to be a miracle
of raspberry taste buds and bladder greens

an ambulance siren
divides the city traffic
he has drowned his organs in poison
and rushes, sperm-swift, towards premeditated death

## III HEART

amplified in the cardiac unit
the businessman's heart is deafening
as the first bang of creation
its valves flap open on a fibreglass moth's wing

artery walls are daubed in cholesterol and smoke
and heart's pothole is choked in clots
curdled blood begins to slake
its insatiable mouth

and it misses the note of life
broadcasting alarm hoarsely
through the loudhailer of stethoscope
its morse tapping an emergency code:

in the operating theatre
light enters tunnels, ventricles, again
heart smacks its rosy lips
revived by a trickling saliva of blood


IV   BRAIN

a fig leaf of skin
hides the shameful serpent of intestines
our parcel of flesh is tied
with nerve ends and veins

over which is coiled
the brain's grey rope
a meaty sandwich spread
a cushioned seat of wisdom

preserved under a cracked ceiling
with the pineal body ('site of the soul')
cloud puffy
dreamy between hemispheres

and sometimes cords are purposely snapped
brain's knotted pâté is sliced
or electric shocks
singe troubling memories


V   EYES

the meaning of breasts is mastectomy
the meaning of liver is cancer
the meaning of chest is asthma
the meaning of eyes is blindness

their jewels embellish head's cup
producing like oysters
the cultured pearls,
the clear water, of tears

the pupil is a black hole
where clusters of burning stars were swallowed
others shine still, fuelled with beauty,
casting eyelash rays

the cornea is our window
on the outside world
hooding flesh that relishes flesh
and is reflected in its lover's gaze

## VI   SKELETON

when tight dress of skin,
a body stocking, is threadbare
and wickerwork of muscle
unwinds from biceps and thigh

like elastic bands, a mummy's covering
our classical interior is revealed
carved bust of skull
marble pillars of bone

and pictures painted in blood fade
from walls of head
knowledge, love and dread are emptied
the meat machine halts production

and salted tide of life ebbs
in which foetus gills thrived
leaving a landscape of calcium rocks
our solid foundation stones

## VII   DEATH

what will be our certified cause of death
will we expire with the lost memory of arteriosclerosis
dissolving in alcohol, crumbling with pain
basted in our own body fat, shivering with old age

our distilled water polluted by cancer, angina, rash
until we resign work and life and suffering
all family fights over, love consummated, arguments resolved
the patiently accumulated facts forgotten:

the red bouquet of heart we offered partners withers
its petalled rose shrivels, its valves harden into thorns
fresh cream of breasts sours, dream topping of skin acidifies
cherry nipples turn to pips

the clock is a wheel of fortune
each second leads to separate destinies, reprieve or death,
its thin hands are the compass needles that direct us
pilot us from time

## VIII    THROUGH THE MICROSCOPE

the long flowing tresses of a fallopian tube
the crazy paving of cells
the stained-glass window of hormone crystals
the abstract canvas of a city dweller's lung

the rainfall of erected hair
the stranded dolphin of a nerve
the flaming snout of the pulmonary vein
the gaping volcanoes of the colon

the butter yellow of cholesterol
the stratified rock of cones and rods
the magnified saliva of a gourmet
the decayed tooth of racial superiority

the drained kidney of ambition
the white vocal cords of politics like gleaming fangs
the roots of wit and sarcasm inexplicable
the binding agent of life still unidentified

# Seán Dunne

b. 1956

## QUAKERS

Silence takes over the room.
As if gathered for a sign, they dispatch
Business and let the moments pass.
On tables, in bowls, flowers bud
Like phrases about to be said.

Outside, their acre of graves shows
Only names and dates like the flat
Covers of shut files. Terraces close
Around them, dogs restless in yards,
Children at windows catapulting birds.

## MESSAGE HOME

*for Sara*

Curving past wards, lawns and avenues teem
With patients strolling to lessen time.
The strands of your hair are split like fine
Tweezers as you stand, I imagine, beside
Curtains the colour of leaves that fall
On wet pavements near a girls' school

Here, the valley presents a picture of peace—
An ordered landscape of tranquil fields,
Barley broken by the flight of crows
Startled by shotguns. Tired of the old
Scene, I read Mother Julian in her cell:
Each page a promise that all shall be well.

But we inhabit a harsher world, our
Lives confined to balconies for an hour
Absorbing the sun to lessen our hurt.
A farmer walks across acres of turned earth
In the distance, appraising each neat lap.
He walks without watching a sinking graph.

Crows flock in thousands here at night,
Each dipping towards its own nest despite
Darkness gathering in a sky that's scaled
Like a mackerel. Somewhere, in massive pain,
A man screams in *delirium tremens*, gross
Birds enlarged in his mind to a roar.

To cope with such pain I pretend you stand
Shelling peas into a white bowl, your hand
Deftly tossing pods aside. Or your hair
In a peasant scarf as you prepare
Dough on a floured table. Like secrets I set
These pictures against this place where death

Is habitual as morning. Wheeled trolleys tell
Of another gone, sheets replaced and all
The charts unclipped. The priest towels
Chrism from his hands and prays aloud.
I think of you sleeping, your tired face,
Banishing the hurt of these times, this place.

# WEDDING-LETTER TO NEW DELHI

*for Dan and Gretta*

Working at my window above the Lee now
Spreading in flood through streets where rain
Poignant as some worn, provincial novel,
Sweeps from grey and dims the flash
Of neon at the nightclub door, I think
Of you in your land of caked earth and thick
Heat where ponderous cattle pass: loud
Laneways of Delhi where echoes hardly ring.

From here to there an infinite journey yet
Hardly longer than any made with pain and risk.
I imagine your wedding—an outdoor altar where
The priest in white vestments talks of home.
Around you the dense silence of the compound
Where servants stare through a bamboo fence,
Eyes fixing details into focus like a lens.
Or else it happens in a crumbling office; some

Fat official flicks flies from a sill before
Rapidly speaking the civic vows, his face
A dark blubber in the heat, his pen
Sticky in your hands when you sign the book.
Afterwards a long meal in a friend's garden,
Someone singing to a low sitar until you join
In songs whose words you can hardly know.
A rustling of beaded curtains and you go.

I live in the wrong time to fill my song with pale
Nymphs who surround you singing *Io! Io! Hymen Io!*
Or to talk of forests where minstrels with pipes
And tabors play to celebrate your act. I offer
What I see from my high window—the still city,
Walls where shredded posters catch the rain,
Doors open in flats along Wellington Road
Where sports results crackle across corridors.

Does this depiction of the real depress your gay
Spirits on this your wedding-day? If so I only
Claim that in such crude pictures lies our proper
Place, that the torn paper trapped in a pool
Or the squeak of an unoiled bicycle after dark
Contain more wonder at the being alive
Than the pined-for, chorus-haunted wood,
The conjured Orpheus with impossible lute.

*With that I saw two Swannes of goodly hewe*
*Come softly swimming down along the Lee,*
Their gaze set on the current's flow, necks
Curled against the dismal showers. Around
Them, cranes turn above anchored ships
And in their perfect poise I find your match:
A measured pace, oriental in its calm.
From here to Delhi let their echoes ring.

## THE BEAN FEAST

Stacked in jars on shelves, the beans
Diminish in time to favourite recipes.
Poured into bowls, the chosen piles
Soak overnight. They burst in darkness
As we sleep, immune to their protest.
As if for a birth, they crack and swell
In cupboards among crockery and herbs.
They soften into life without a sound.

Their names contain them like gloves:
Red kidney beans, skins open and loose,
Or moong beans, pellets of hard seed.
The blackeye watches us behind glass
And butter beans are smooth as cobbles.
The speckled pintos, the round haricots—
Stones for jewelry, pebbles or beads.
The kitchen answers to their every need.

What if they hear us at night, our low
Whispers aching for comprehension, sighs
They yearn to decipher? Old favourites
Of the earth, they have little to learn.
At times I sense them soaking in the dark,
Swelling towards the glimmer of moonlight
Between hinges of the pantry door. Cold
Multitudes, they absorb our lives as well.

# Notes on Contributors

MICHAEL COADY was born in Carrick-on-Suir, Co. Tipperary, in 1939. He is now a teacher there. In 1979, he won the Patrick Kavanagh Award for poetry. He also writes short stories. A collection of his poems, *Two for a Woman, Three for a Man*, was published in 1980.

PÁDRAIG J. DALY was born in Dungarvan, Co. Waterford, in 1943. An Augustinian priest, his books of poetry are *Nowhere But In Praise* (1978), *This Day's Importance* (1981) and *A Celibate Affair* (1984). His work has also been published in Italy.

MICHAEL DAVITT was born in Cork in 1950. He now lives in Dublin. He is founder-editor of *Innti*, a magazine of new poetry in Irish. *Gleann Ar Ghleann*, his first collection of poems, was published in 1981; his second, *Bligeard Sráide*, appeared in 1983.

SEÁN DUNNE was born in Waterford in 1956. He now lives in Cork where he works as a freelance writer. His poems have been widely published in Ireland and elsewhere, and a number appear in *Raven Introductions I* (1983). His first collection appears from Dolmen Press in 1985.

PAUL DURCAN was born in Co. Mayo, in 1944. He now lives in Cork where, for a time, he was editor of *The Cork Review*. He won the Patrick Kavanagh Award in 1974. His main collections of poetry are *O Westport In the Light of Asia Minor* (1975), *Teresa's Bar* (1976), *Sam's Cross* (1978), *Jesus, Break His Fall* (1981), *Ark of the North* (1982), *The Selected Paul Durcan* (ed. Edna Longley, 1982) and *Jumping the Train Tracks with Angela* (1984).

JOHN ENNIS was born in Co. Westmeath in 1944. He won the Patrick Kavanagh Award in 1975. He is Head of the Department of Humanities at the Regional Technical College in Waterford. His books are *Night on Hibernia* (1976), *Dolmen Hill* (1977) and *A Drink of Spring* (1979).

PATRICK GALVIN was born in Cork in 1929. He served for a time in the French Foreign Legion. His collections of poetry are *Heart of Grace* (1957), *Christ in London* (1960), *The Wood-Burners* (1973) and *Man on a Porch* (1980). Seven of his plays have been staged in Belfast and Dublin; he also writes plays for radio. He was resident dramatist at the Lyric Theatre, Belfast from 1974–8.

MICHAEL HARTNETT/MICHEÁL Ó HAIRTNÉIDE was born in Co. Limerick in 1941. For many years he lived in Dublin before returning to Co. Limerick. He originally wrote in English but in 1975 he announced that Irish was to be his medium. His books include *Anatomy of a Cliché* (1968), *Selected Poems* (1970), *A Farewell to English* (1975), *Adharca Broic* (1978) and *An Phurgóid* (1983). *Collected Poems* Volume I, his poems in English, appeared in 1984.

BRENDAN KENNELLY was born in Co. Kerry, 1936. Professor of Modern Literature at Trinity College, Dublin, he won the A.E. Memorial Award in 1967. His many books include *Good Souls To Survive* (1967), *A Kind of Trust* (1975), *New and Selected Poems* (1976), *The Boats Are Home* (1980) and *Cromwell* (1983). He has also written two novels, *The Crooked Cross* (1963) and *The Florentines* (1967). He edited *The Penguin Book of Irish Verse* (1970).

SEÁN LUCY was born in Bombay, 1931. Professor of Modern English at University College, Cork, since 1967. He has edited *Love Poems of the Irish* (1967) and *Five Irish Poets* (1970). A collection of poems, *Unfinished Sequence*, appeared in 1979.

THOMAS MCCARTHY was born in Co. Waterford in 1954. He won the Patrick Kavanagh Award in 1977 and was a Fellow of the International Writing Program at the University of Iowa in 1978–9. His books are *The First Convention* (1978), *The Sorrow Garden* (1981) and *The Non-Aligned Storyteller* (1984). He lives and works in Cork.

THOMAS MACGREEVY was born in Co. Kerry in 1893. He fought in the First World War, and later lived in Paris and London. He was Director of the National Gallery in Dublin for some years. He died in 1967. His *Poems* appeared in 1934. *Collected Poems* (1971) was reissued in the Belacqua Series in 1983.

AIDAN MURPHY was born in Cork, 1952. He now lives in

London. A selection from his poems appeared in *Raven Introductions I* (1983); his first collection, *The Restless Factor*, was published in 1985.

LIAM MURPHY was born in Waterford in 1948. A book of his poems, *Occasion of Wordshed*, was published in 1970. He lives and works in Waterford.

EILÉAN NÍ CHUILLEANÁIN was born in Cork in 1942. She lectures in English at Trinity College, Dublin. She won the Patrick Kavanagh Award in 1973 for her first book *Acts and Monuments*. She is a co-editor of *Cyphers*, a literary magazine. Her other books are *Site of Ambush* (1975), *The Second Voyage* (1977), *Cork* (with Brian Lalor, 1977) and *The Rose-Geranium* (1981).

NUALA NÍ DHOMHNAILL was born in England in 1952, of Co. Kerry parents. She lived for some years in Turkey but now lives in Ireland. A collection of poems *An Dealg Droighin* was published in 1981. She has also written short stories.

FRANK O'CONNOR is the pseudonym of Michael O'Donovan, born in Cork in 1903. Best known as a writer of short stories, he also translated extensively from the Irish. He died in 1966. His books include *Guests of the Nation* (1931) and *Three Old Brothers* (1936). His translations from the Irish are included in *Kings, Lords and Commons* (1959) and *The Little Monasteries* (1963).

GREGORY O'DONOGHUE was born in Cork in 1951. He lived in Canada for a short time and now lives in England. *Kicking*, a collection of poems, appeared in 1975.

ROBERT O'DONOGHUE was born in Cork in 1929. He works as a journalist and drama critic with the *Cork Examiner*. His poems have appeared in many publications. Also a dramatist, his plays include *The Long Night* and *Hate Was The Spur*.

DENNIS O'DRISCOLL was born in Co. Tipperary in 1954. He has contributed poetry and criticism to many publications, including *Agenda*, *Quarto* and *The Sunday Tribune*. He lives in Dublin. His first collection of poems *Kist* was published in 1982.

DESMOND O'GRADY was born in Co. Limerick in 1935. He has travelled widely and translated from many languages. He lives in Co. Cork and spends summers on the Greek island of Paros. His books include *Reilly* (1961), *The Dark Edge of Europe* (1967), *The Dying Gaul* (1968), *His Skaldcrane's Nest* (1979) and *The Headgear of the Tribe* (1979).

SEÁN Ó RÍORDÁIN was born in Co. Cork in 1917. Considered by many to be the most important contemporary poet to write in Irish, he was also a columnist with *The Irish Times* for some years. His diaries, excerpts from which have appeared in various publications, are also of great interest. He died in 1977. His books include *Eireaball Spideoige* (1952), *Brosna* (1964) and *Línte Liombó* (1971).

SEÁN Ó TUAMA was born in Cork in 1926. Professor of Modern Literature in Irish at University College, Cork. His books include *Moloney* (1966), *Saol Fó Thoinn* (1978) and *Filí Faoi Sceimhle* (1978). With Thomas Kinsella, he edited the bilingual anthology *An Duanaire 1600–1900: Poems of the Dispossessed* (1981).

MAURICE RIORDAN was born in Co. Cork in 1953. He has lived in Canada and England, and has been a poetry reviewer for *The Irish Press*. His poems have mainly appeared in magazines and journals.

AUGUSTUS YOUNG was born in Cork in 1943. He now lives in England. His works include *On Loaning Hill* (1972), *Rosemaries* (1976), *Tapestry of Animals* (1977), *The Credit, Book I* (1980) and *The Credit, Book II* (1985). *Danta Grádha*, translations from the Irish, appeared in 1975. He is also a playwright.

# Acknowledgements

I am happy to acknowledge the assistance I received from the following in compiling this anthology: Seán Bohan and Kieran Burke of the Cork City Library; Diarmuid Ó Drisceoil; the staff of the Triskel Arts Centre, and especially Anne O'Sullivan; Sara Gavin; John Montague, who introduced me to Mangan's anthology, which in turn led to the idea of this one.

S.D.

The editor and publishers wish to thank the poets, their representatives and publishers as follows for permission to include copyright material.

For poems by MICHAEL COADY: The Gallery Press, Dublin for 'Second Honeymoon', 'Two for a Woman, Three for a Man' and 'Oh No, 'Twas the Truth' from *Two for a Woman, Three for a Man* (1980).

For poems by PÁDRAIG J. DALY: Profile Press, Dublin for 'Summers in Doneraile' from *Nowhere But in Praise* (1978); Raven Arts Press, Dublin for 'Coolroe' from *This Day's Importance* (1981).

For poems by MICHAEL DAVITT: Sáirséal Ó Marcaigh, Dublin for 'Meirg Agus Lios Luachra', 'Seandaoine', 'I gCuimhne Ar Lís Ceárnaighe, Blascaodach' from *Gleann Ar Ghleann* (1981); Coiscéim, Dublin for 'An Scáthán' from *Bligeard Sráide* (1983); Faber and Faber, London for 'The Mirror' translated by Paul Muldoon in *Quoof* (1983); the author for his translations.

For poems by SEÁN DUNNE: Raven Arts Press for 'Wedding-Letter to New Delhi', 'Quakers' and 'Message Home' from *Raven Introductions I* (1983); the author for 'The Bean Feast'.

For poems by PAUL DURCAN: Blackstaff Press, Belfast for 'Protestant Old Folks' Coach Tour of County Kerry', 'The Difficulty That Is Marriage', 'She Mends an Ancient Wireless', 'The Weeping Headstones of the Isaac Becketts', 'Memoirs of a Fallen Blackbird', 'Making Love Outside Áras An Uachtaráin' and 'The Married Man Who Fell in

Love with a Semi-State Body' from *The Selected Paul Durcan* (1982); Profile Press for 'The Pregnant Proprietress of the Fish and Chipper' from *Sam's Cross* (1978); Raven Arts Press and Carcanet Press, Manchester for 'The Problem of Fornication on The Blarney Chronicle' from *Jumping the Train Tracks with Angela* (1984); Raven Arts Press for 'The Death by Heroin of Sid Vicious' from *Jesus Break His Fall* (1981).

For poems by JOHN ENNIS: The Gallery Press for 'Sgarúint na gCompánach' from *Night on Hibernia* (1976), 'Birth at Airmount' from *Dolmen Hill* (1977), 'A Drink of Spring', 'Holy Hour', 'Bad Friday' and 'All Over' from *A Drink of Spring* (1979); the author for 'Strand Dump at Irishtown'.

For poems by PATRICK GALVIN: New Writers' Press, Dublin for 'Miss Cecily Finch' and 'The Madwoman of Cork' from *The Wood-Burners* (1973); Martin, Brian & O'Keeffe, London for 'Little Red Knife', 'Plaisir d'Amour', 'The Bard', 'The Aunt', 'Advice to a Poet' and 'Message to the Editor' from *Man on the Porch* (1980).

For poems by MICHAEL HARTNETT/MICHEÁL Ó HAIRTNÉIDE: The Gallery Press for 'Ssu K'ung T'u Walks in the Forest', 'I saw magic on a green country road...', 'The Oat Woman', 'Pigkilling', 'Death of an Irish Woman' and the extracts from 'A Farewell to English' and 'The Retreat of Ita Cagney' from *A Farewell to English* (1978); Raven Arts Press and Carcanet Press for 'I have exhausted the delighted range...' from *Collected Poems* Volume I (1984); Goldsmith Press, Dublin for an excerpt from 'Cúlú Íde' from *Adharca Broic* (1978).

For poems by BRENDAN KENNELLY: Allen Figgis & Co., Dublin for 'Blackbird' from *Good Souls to Survive* (1967); The Gallery Press for 'The Gift', 'The Swimmer', 'The Tippler', 'My Dark Feathers', 'Bread' and 'A Kind of Trust' from *New and Selected Poems* (1976), 'We are Living' from *The Boats Are Home* (1980).

For poems by SEÁN LUCY: The Mercier Press, Cork for 'Longshore Intellectual' from *Five Irish Poets* (1970); Wolfhound Press, Dublin for 'Donal Ogue' and the excerpts from 'Unfinished Sequence for Seán Ó Riada' from *Unfinished Sequence* (1979).

For poems by THOMAS MCCARTHY: The Dolmen Press, Portlaoise for 'State Funeral', 'Daedalus, The Maker' and 'The Rarest Thyme' from *The First Convention* (1978); Anvil Press Poetry, London for 'The Provincial Writer's Diary', 'The Sorrow Garden' and 'Her Widowhood' from *The Sorrow Garden* (1981), 'Party Shrine' and 'André Gide' from *The Non-Aligned Storyteller* (1984).

For poems by THOMAS MACGREEVY: Raven Arts Press and New Writers' Press for 'De Civitate Hominum', 'Homage to Hieronymus Bosch', 'Aodh Ruadh Ó Domhnaill', 'Homage to Marcel Proust', 'Recessional',

'Nocturne of the Self-Evident Presence', 'Gioconda' and 'On the Death of Joseph Djugashvli *alias* Stalin' from *Collected Poems* (1971, 1983).

For poems by AIDAN MURPHY: Raven Arts Press for 'Friendship', 'Memorial Albert Camus' and 'Whistling' from *Raven Introductions I* (1983); the author for 'Elegy for a Bride'.

For poems by LIAM MURPHY: *The Irish Press* and David Marcus for 'Good Friday 1982'; Tara Telephone Publications, Dublin for 'For Fear of Waking the Alarm Clock' from *Occasion of Wordshed* (1970).

For poems by EILÉAN Ní CHUILLEANÁIN: The Gallery Press for "Lucina Schynning in Silence of the Nicht ...", 'Wash', 'Swineherd', 'The Second Voyage' and 'Going Back to Oxford' from *Acts and Monuments* (1972), 'The Lady's Tower', 'Old Roads' and 'Odysseus Meets the Ghosts of the Women' from *Site of Ambush* (1975), 'A Gentleman's Bedroom' from *The Rose-Geranium* (1981).

For poems by NUALA Ní DHOMHNAILL: The Mercier Press for 'Leaba Shíoda', 'Mór Goraí', 'I mBaile An tSléibhe', 'Na Súile Uaine', 'Venio ex Oriente' and 'Ní féidir liom lui anseo níos mó ...' from *An Dealg Droighin* (1981); Raven Arts Press for 'Venio ex Oriente' and 'I cannot lie here anymore ...' translated by Michael Hartnett from *Raven Introductions 3* (1984); the author for her translations.

For poems by FRANK O'CONNOR: A. D. Peters & Co. Ltd and Joan Daves, New York for 'A Sleepless Night' and 'Last Lines' from *Kings, Lords and Commons* (1959) and 'On the Death of His Wife' from *The Little Monasteries* (1963).

For poems by GREGORY O'DONOGHUE: The Gallery Press for 'Mathematician', 'Secret Blessing', 'Globe' and 'The Glass' from *Kicking* (1975); the author for 'Anna Akhmatova' and 'A Nomad'; U.C.C.'s *Quarryman* for 'Aquarium'.

For poems by ROBERT O'DONOGHUE: the author for 'The Witness' and 'Don Juan'.

For poems by DENNIS O'DRISCOLL: The Dolmen Press for 'Departures', 'Village', 'Someone' and 'Being' from *Kist* (1982).

For poems by DESMOND O'GRADY: New Writers' Press for the extract from *Hellas* (1971); The Gallery Press for 'The Poet in Old Age Fishing at Evening', 'Sightseeing', the extract from 'The Dark Edge of Europe', 'Reading the Unpublished Manuscripts of Louis MacNeice at Kinsale Harbour', 'Professor Kelleher and the Charles River', 'Afternoon' and 'The Old Ways' from *The Headgear of the Tribe* (1979).

For poems by SEÁN Ó RíORDÁIN: Sáirséal Ó Marcaigh for 'Adhlacadh Mo Mháthar', 'Cnoc Melleri' and 'Cúl An Tí' from *Eireaball Spideoige* (1952), 'Claustrophobia', 'Reo', 'Fiabhras' and 'Na Leamhain' from *Brosna* (1964), 'Ceol Ceantair' from *Línte Liombó* (1971).

For poems by SEÁN Ó TUAMA: An Clóchomhar, Dublin for 'Cá Síulfam', 'Rousseau Na Gaeltachta' and 'Ise Seachtó hOcht, Eisean Ochtó Ceathair' from *Saol Fó Thoinn* (1978); the author for original and translation of "Besides, Who Knows Before the End What Sun May Shine", and his other translations.

For poems by MAURICE RIORDAN: the author for 'The Drift' and 'Pursuit'.

For poems by AUGUSTUS YOUNG: New Writers' Press for 'Heritage' and 'Last Refuge' from *On Loaning Hill* (1972); the author for excerpts from 'Mr Thackeray on Cork'.

# Index of Poets